IN MY FATHER'S GARDEN

A Deep South Book

IN MY FATHER'S GARDEN

Lee May

THE UNIVERSITY OF ALABAMA PRESS

Tuscaloosa and London

Originally published by Longstreet Press, 1995
Paperback edition published by The University of Alabama Press, 2002
The University of Alabama Press
Tuscaloosa, Alabama 35487-0380
Manufactured in the United States of America

Portions of this work first appeared in the *Atlanta Journal-Constitution* and *Essence.*

9 8 7 6 5 4 3 2 1
10 09 08 07 06 05 04 03 02

Typeface is ACaslon.

∞
The paper on which this book is printed meets the minimum requirements of American National Standard for Information Science–Permanence of Paper for Printed Library Materials, ANSI Z39.48–1984.

Catalog-in-Publication data available from the Library of Congress

ISBN 0-8173-1158-0

British Library Cataloguing-in-Publication Data available

For my father, after so many years;
For Mother and Dad, my role models for life;
And for Lyn, naturally, and our blending family

Meridian, Mississippi
June 20, 1989

The narrow concrete walkway stretches barely twenty feet from the street to the porch, but this nervous-making visit made the distance seem more like a mile.

I had come to my father's home. Once, it was mine, too. On this scorching, Mississippi-dusty June day, the house on 30th Avenue seemed one of the few things in life that had not changed; it still was small. Two bedrooms, a kitchen and living room, its shell sheathed in those white asbestos shingles. On the faded burgundy-painted concrete floor sat two green metal chairs, the kind that spring back and forth as you rock your body.

Getting out of my little rental car, I peered up the walk to see my father, sitting still in one of the chairs. He was wearing a tiny smile, a light-colored shirt and newish overalls that floated around his body. He seemed so old. And so thin. So changed.

No wonder, I told myself as I yelled, "Hey! How ya doin'?" and started the long walk toward the porch. No wonder. Now, June 20, 1989, it had been thirty-nine years since I was last at this house. And since I last saw my father, eighty years old by this time. I was forty-eight.

"I'm doing tolerable well. How you?" Ples Mae answered. During those decades in which I had not seen him, whenever I thought of him, I always wondered about his name. His first name is pronounced *Plez*, and his last name is spelled differently from mine. Someday, I would always think, I'll find out why.

But that could wait. It was time to walk that mile, a journey through almost four decades, through tons of events, memories and lives. My father and my mother, Riller, split up in 1950, when I, their only child, was nine. They both remarried. He to Mary Sterdivant, she to Milton Walker, the man I called Dad. The word stepfather would not have done him justice. My mother and dad and I moved from Meridian to East St. Louis, Illinois, in 1955, severing all contact with my father. Funny how seeing him after all these years recalled memories of my other two parents. Ironic that this was the eve of what would have been my mother's sixty-seventh birthday.

As I reached the porch, I did not know what to expect. Would we hug? We did not. My father did not rise. We shook hands. I sat. On one level this first meeting went as if we had seen each other just days before. There was no rush of questions about the past, no obvious look to gauge what the years had done. Weirdly, it was natural. How could we possibly catch the years we had lost? Better to go from now.

But Mary was much more demonstrative. She rushed through the door with a large grin and yelled, "Sonny! Sonny! I'm so glad you're here to see your Daddy! You don't know how many years I've prayed for this to happen." My father looked a little sheepish as Mary, a thinly built woman, hard of hearing but not hard to hear, darted back inside the house, talking over her shoulder: "Y'all talk. Go on and talk. I'm fixing dinner. Sonny, you got to eat something. We got butter beans outta the garden. Frozen fresh."

Just as I was unprepared for him to be so old, I also did not expect to see so much of myself in him. I noted that we were about the same height, six feet, and our facial structures, along with balding hair pattern, showed our connections.

Physical similarities aside, we had lived two disparate lives, worlds apart in many ways. Mine had been spread over many addresses, while most of my father's had unfolded right here. Sitting on the front porch, we made small talk to try bridging that time gap. I looked out onto 30th Avenue, then across the street, trying to recapture long-lost memories of my years in this neighborhood.

Searching for lost memories of my father, I felt a flush of discomfort and doubt. Was it really possible to make any meaning of a relationship that had not existed for forty years? Was coming here a bad idea after all?

"Been a hot one today," I said, wiping my forehead. "Hadn't been much rain."

"Yeah, I been having to water every day."

After about half an hour that felt like much longer, Mary appeared at the front door, calling us in to a wonderfully intoxicating meal—gifts from the garden. Around noonday, this meal was dinner to many Southerners, while the meal I would eat later, around 7 p.m., was supper. As Mary had advertised, there were butter beans mixed with peas, tomatoes, collards, okra, and corn bread, washed down with sodas.

Pretty soon, we took a stroll, to see what he was having to water. I was amazed at how orderly was his garden, rows straight and clean as arrows.

"Those tomatoes oughta be ready to eat any day," I said.

"If the squirrels don't get 'em first," he replied.

That first walk in my father's garden was filled with so much of my past. In that space, that deep, narrow lot, I could see the cages of rabbits that had infatuated me as a child, revolted me when I realized we were supposed to eat them. My dachshund, Pup Pup, had trotted from one end of the lot to the other, under the cages, among the vegetables.

And just as it had done almost forty years earlier, the sun-drenched garden grew just about everything a family might need. Collards, corn, butter beans, peas, tomatoes, peppers, squash, watermelon, potatoes. And, amazingly, peanuts, their vines twirling out of a network of old car tires. Proudly, my father pointed out each crop, giving me a rundown on its progress, how well he expected it to bear.

"Now, this okra gonna make more than we can eat," he said in a voice that combined deep tones and heavy punctuations, one that must reflect something from his western Alabama upbringing. "And we gonna freeze these butter beans and peas, 'cause we get so many. Always do. We eat 'em all year long."

From the peanuts in the front of the garden, near the house, to the gnarled grapevine at the garden's end, near the spot where mosses and ferns grow in the wet, we walked during that visit and each subsequent one, looking, talking—a lot about gardening but also about my journalism career, neighbors long gone and half forgotten, politics, his health; he had long suffered from high blood pressure, alerting me to a danger I had feared for years, as mine had been borderline.

We must have been in the garden for about thirty minutes when he introduced me to his garden shed. A small corrugated-tin structure near the house, it contained the usual assortment of hoes, picks, shovels and trowels. All were clean and oiled. There also was a monstrous gasoline-powered plow that he was to later offer me—an offer I took as a huge measure of affection but had to decline as my space would not accommodate it.

Suddenly, my father grabbed a BB gun that was leaning against the shed's wall. Striding a few feet from the shed, he turned and fired, "Ping!," striking a tin can fifteen paces away. The proud father had shown off, just as his son might have forty years earlier. "You got to be able to shoot straight to get them rats," he said, all but blowing across the top of the gun barrel. I was impressed.

I was glad that I had come.

I had decided to reach out to my father when a writing assignment brought me from Washington, D.C., where I was living, to Meridian. The story centered on the twenty-fifth anniversary of the murders of three civil rights workers in nearby Philadelphia, Mississippi.

Also, I knew then that my wife, Lyn, and I would in a few weeks be moving from Washington to Atlanta, as I was being promoted from correspondent in the *Los Angeles Times* Washington bureau to chief of its Southern bureau. This meant that my father and I would be only three hundred miles apart.

But such practical reasons were nothing compared to the emotional ones. I wanted some questions answered. Who is this man? Would seeing him show me what I might become? Could I learn what afflictions might strike me? Should I worry about my borderline high blood pressure, my over-two-hundred cholesterol?

As Mother and Dad both were dead, shouldn't I have some sort of relationship with my sole surviving parent?

I had looked up his telephone number and made the call, knowing that this could backfire, that I might be awakening a bad relationship. Through all the years, he never wrote, phoned or tried to visit. And neither did I. Why is impossible to know. Fear of rejection? Pride? Anger? Fear of nothing to say? Fear of intrusion? When I got him on the phone, neither of us brought up the whys.

And we did not bring them up during the visit. Nor did we confront one another about the gulf that so long separated us.

I hoped that our meeting would represent a kind of closure, or at least the beginning of one, resolving questions about what kind of father and son we might have been.

We met much like two strangers, but strangers with a history. In a couple of hours, we touched on highlights of the previous thirty-some years. It seemed unrealistic to reach for more than highlights at that time.

Then, visit by visit, talk by talk, we found kinship in our love for growing plants, gradually expanding that to include other parts of our lives. This first meeting, tough as it started out to be, was the start of something tender.

DOWN HOME, UP SOUTH

Gardens, like women, have been a part of my life always, even before I learned to call their names.

In Cuba, Alabama, the little bump in the road twenty miles east of Meridian, where I was born Eddie Lee May in a drafty log cabin more than half a century ago, we used to call our growing spaces "yards." Back yard. Front yard. And any plant you grew but didn't eat was a "flower." As for vegetables, each simply was called by its name. Collards, corn, tomatoes, watermelons, squash, butter beans and much more grew in the yards of my childhood—the first belonging to my mother's mother, Mary Reed, my Big Momma. She raised my mother, Riller, and ten other children, partly alone as her husband had died before my mother, the youngest, was born.

"I'm going out and pick some peas," Big Momma would say, not, "I'm going to the garden and pick some peas."

In a long flour-sack, flower-patterned dress, fronted with an apron, this slight, smooth-skinned woman, barely five feet tall, head wrapped in a plain kerchief, would wade through the waist-high okra in weed-free rows to the perfect purple-hull peas, which would be shelled a few hours later in a family gathering on the porch (without my father, who was in the Army).

Surely, something about gardening made her gentle, and patient beyond imagination. How else to account for her always heeding my petulant four-year-old's demand to "cook me some flapjacks" on her hulking cast-iron stove?

Mortified at my nagging and tugging, my mother tried to get me to lighten up, pointing out that Big Momma already had her hands full, cooking a meal for who knows how many folks. But Big Momma would just chuckle and say, "That's all right; I'll cook that baby some flapjacks."

Big Momma was unflappable most times, but she, like my mother, was deeply disturbed when, a few months later, I tried to play in the fire under her iron washpot cooking clothes in the backyard and burned my feet so badly that I was confined to a crib enclosed in screen wire to prevent the flies from covering the wounds. Big Momma would hover around the crib, fretting and blaming herself, salving my spirit and dressing my wounds.

It was she who introduced me to herbal medicine, brewing pine needle tea to fight colds and using the giant fuzzy leaves and flowers of the mullein plant to make a brew that fought coughs. Big Momma had plenty of opportunity to perfect her brews in a house whose many cracks and holes let us see the sky and the earth and sent us shivering to bed after baths in a galvanized tin washtub.

And it was she who soothed my mother, an inexperienced parent in her early twenties, counseling her not to worry, when the horse I had climbed upon galloped off down the road, despite the shouts and chases of a half-dozen relatives. Sure enough, we came back, unscathed, proud of the adventure. At least I was.

I was in no shape to know, but I imagine neither of them was soothable when my Uncle Buddy, Mother's oldest brother, my mentor in decadence, took me off on one of his jaunts to the woods and allowed me (I barely reached his knees) to roll my own Prince Albert cigarettes and swig from a bottle of moonshine until I passed out.

According to Mother, I slept for twenty-four hours, while Buddy and Big Momma stared at me, with Buddy repeatedly promising: "Lord, if you let Uncle Pop wake up, I'll never give him another drink." Of course, he did not keep the promise, although he was careful to never again give me enough to knock me out.

Big Momma died when I was about ten years old. But she made a lifetime impression on me, showing me that a strong character and a rich spirit have the power to lift lives out of the lowliest circumstances and make them soar. That lesson, taught simply by the joy she found and shared in life, was passed on to her daughter, my mother. The two of them, kind and loving without coddling (the flapjack thing notwithstanding), represented my happy introduction to women and to gardening—two wonderful elements of my life that sometimes have taken center stage simultaneously and at other times played their roles alternately.

My father's parents died before I was born, but he has spoken lovingly of his mother, Cora, who instilled in him a sense of fierce pride and independence. After serving in the Army, he worked in sawmills around Cuba for a while. Then, when I was about five years old, he moved us from Big Momma's house to Meridian, a virtual metropolis, relatively speaking. Fortunately, I was able to make frequent trips back and even was allowed to feed the chickens and slop the hogs and, when the cold came, see them slaughtered for meat that was cured in the smokehouse.

What a huge change this new house was: a bathtub instead of the washtub set by the fireplace on Saturday night. And in no room could I look up to see the stars or down to see the ground.

Kindergarten at Baptist Seminary in Meridian was a wonderful blur of afternoon naps and cookies and milk, but elementary school at Wechsler was notable for one reason: Willie Earl was one of my classmates.

Willie Earl was the biggest fourth-grader at Wechsler, six

School Days
1947-48

Young Eddie Lee. Ples on porch during that first visit.

feet tall. I don't know how old he was, chronologically, but he was in many ways younger than most of us nine- and ten-year-olds. He would cry when young bully boys taunted him for his inability to read or spell.

But he would recover when those same bullies marveled at his ability to multiply, add or divide three-digit numbers. Later, I came to think of Willie Earl as an idiot savant, a gentle giant. But at the time, he was just that big boy whose nose was always running and who always seemed frightened.

I do not know whatever became of Willie Earl, but I always hoped that he wound up living lavishly, making money in gambling casinos with his mathematical talent, like some kind of Rain Man. Whatever his fate, I owe him for helping me understand eventually that the mind holds mysteries that eyes can never see.

Between school times, back in the neighborhood, my best buddy across the street, Bobby, and I were busy pursuing other concerns. Why, for instance, clay dirt tasted so good. We would dig it out of the side of a little hill next door to Bobby, then sit on a ridge and devour it. I do not know how we came to seek out this delicacy, having no recollection of anyone's recommending it; I've always wondered whether there really is some genetic Southern thing that leads us to behavior like that.

Tutored by an older boy in the neighborhood, Bobby and I worked constantly on our golf games, played on a lot next to his house with discarded broomsticks for clubs and the prickly fruit of the sweet gum tree for balls. I have never been able to look at a sweet gum without thinking, "Fore!"

As far as I could tell, we were a good family, having a good time. My father, who became a plumber after learning the trade through the GI Bill, earned enough money to buy the little white house. My mother, "Muddear" to me until I was in my teens, then Mother, made the house a home, and from time to time worked outside it. At one point she ran an elevator in a downtown office—thrilling me endlessly on those occasions when she'd let me drive the thing and stop it by turning a brass handle as we approached the floor.

My mother, who was short, five feet tall, and round, often weighing close to two hundred pounds, had a sense of humor and joy about life to match her size. The smooth brownness of her face was enriched by her smile, which could heal the nastiest of knee scrapes or melt the chilliest heart of a stranger. Muddear and I would laugh and laugh when I first started steering the elevator and would stop it about half a foot above or below the floor.

"Boy, you ain't never going to learn to run this thing," she would say. Or, if she wanted to get my attention quickly, she'd use my first and middle names, Eddie Lee, as in, "Eddie Lee, quit messing with that elevator; you know you don't know what you're doing." (I dropped Eddie in 1973, while in graduate school.)

Many years later, I dismissed her efforts to learn to drive a car in the same way, secretly hoping she would prove me wrong. She did, as I did with her and the elevator. In both cases, we set our jaws, learned to drive and had great laughs afterward.

I never thought about how or why we never laughed and had much fun at home. There, the three of us were rarely jovial, but that was nothing to think about for a kid who'd had a full day on the links.

Nevertheless, family trouble was brewing well out of my eyesight and earshot. Muddear and I moved out. Soon after, she and Milton Walker were married. All before I turned ten years old. The three of us moved across town, to the west side of Meridian, and out of my father's life. Little did I know that when we left, I would not see him again for thirty-nine years.

Muddear's new husband, now my Dad, a muscular man, about five feet eight inches tall, strong physically and gentle emotionally, never made me feel I should not visit my biological father. At the same time, he made it perfectly clear that he was ready to be my father in every other way. (He also had three sons by a previous marriage, and they visited from time to time for a couple of years and then drifted away permanently.)

Using food as a metaphor for whatever needs I might have, Dad told Muddear, "As long as I eat, Sonny eats." Muddear told me about that declaration many years after my boyhood nickname had faded. That simple promise remains my prime example of an expression of commitment.

Dad and Muddear brought joy to one another's lives and to mine. In our new home, there was laughter. And hugging and kissing, the kind of affection that I believe builds strength, character and goodwill in children, both when they get it directly and when they see parents giving it to each other. All my life, I'll never forget my mother's asking me for "some sugar" when I was a little boy, then kissing me on my cheek before I could run, her affectionate pinching my butt and shouting, "Pony meat, pony meat," which always made me squeal with laughter and race around the room.

And the smells. The smells tell a tale.

My mother seemed to cook more in our new life. Not totally a good thing, considering her weight and high blood pressure. But, true to the Southern character—that part of us that makes us drink too much, talk too much and too loud, smoke too much—we were excessive, eating too much food that was too greasy, too salty, too fat. We are rhododendrons: huge showy blooms in bold colors.

In some ways, how we ate and eat reflects the richness of the region. I believe the South still is the most dynamic part of America, an emotional frontier, coming to terms with its relatively new economic desirability even as it lives down the shame of its segregated past.

Ironically, even as Jim Crow reigned during my Mississippi childhood, black people and white people had integrated stomachs; soul food had no color. A mess of collards, a plate of fried chicken and a skillet of pot-likker-soaked cornbread always have bridged the racial gap. At least it was bridged superficially, temporarily. Before restaurants were integrated, many white people ate food at home cooked by black women, the same kind of food they cooked for their own families. Then, after integration, black people and white people began eating it together, publicly.

Unfortunately, most of this stomach integration remains public and usually does not extend to private lives. Black and white office workers might join one another for lunch at soul food eateries, but they've always been less likely to repeat these meals at one another's homes.

But when this does happen, it can bond.

In the mid-1980s, when I was a correspondent in the Washington bureau of the *Los Angeles Times*, another bureau member, Paul Houston, and I struck up a friendship, gravitating toward each other perhaps because we shared the knowledge that, even in Washington, journalism and government and political power were not life.

As it was for me, life for Paul, who died of cancer in 1994, was enjoying personal pleasures. One that we enjoyed together was food. A native North Carolinian, Paul approached eating with great deliberation and at the same time with abandon.

On assignment together in St. Louis, we visited my mother, across the Mississippi River in East St. Louis, Illinois. As was her practice, Mother always cooked twenty pounds of chitlins for me when I went to see her—her version of the fatted calf. On this occasion, she expressed some concern that our white guest may not be a chitlin man. "Maybe I should fix him something else," she said.

She need not have given it a thought. This may not have been Paul's first food choice that day, but he dived in as if it were, keeping up with me and making an anxious mother feel good.

For years, we all talked about that meal, which, of course, was much more than a meal. Paul and I shared many other meals — some of which he prepared. Maybe it is because eating is such a basic need and a personal delight, but whatever the reason, sharing and enjoying a meal with somebody of another color makes you believe that racial harmony really is possible.

In my childhood, harmony was not the issue for me. Just pure pleasure. Greens, garden-fresh, as were the peas, butter beans, squash and a million other vegetables, corn bread, any fried meat, sliced tomatoes all seasoned the air in my mother's kitchen, speaking forever of our eating delights.

Outside also were smells that last forever. Strangely, hot asphalt was among them, a heavy smell that indicated progress, a dirt road being paved in 1950s Meridian. Moving on up. Even more strangely, we neighborhood children ran delightedly behind the truck that sprayed for mosquitoes, up and down our streets, inhaling the clouds of insecticide as if they were cumulus perfumes.

And it was not for nothing that Mississippi was nicknamed the Magnolia State. These stately, leather-leaved trees bloomed profusely in my Meridian summers, their moonlight-white, lemon-scented blooms forever signifying youth anxious to be spent.

In our tiny bathroom, in a five-gallon crock pot, there was the pungent smell of a drink that Mother made, a kind of *sake*, containing rice, yeast, sometimes potatoes, sometimes corn, raisins, oranges and water. She brewed it in the bathroom, sometimes in the kitchen, because those were likely to be the warmest places in the house, speeding the brewing of a drink that was not "cooked" and because in those rooms other odors would mask the mixture's powerful smell.

Mother called her brew tequila. I never tried to correct her. She made this concoction for more than forty years, earning the right to call it anything she wanted to call it.

By any name, it was potent. Over the years I saw many a good drinker keel over after a couple of glasses of Muddear's tequila. And, yes, I have fallen to its hammer-blow, loving the taste, fearing the consequence. The most impressive demonstration of the drink's power was in what it did to Uncle Buddy, a man of supreme dignity. Heavyset, with an infectious laugh, Buddy, a home barber, loved good cigars and elegant leather belts. His neat haircut and clean shave defied the stereotype of the barber who always looked raggedy about the head.

For his outside job, Buddy was a chauffeur, a relatively high-status job for a black man in Cuba in the 1940s and 1950s. Sometimes, when he drove his employer from Cuba into Meridian, he would stop by our house while she went shopping. One hot day, he showed up when a particularly good batch of tequila was just maturing. Buddy knocked back a couple of glasses and, without warning, pushed back from the kitchen table, strode out the front door into the yard, assumed a wide-legged stance and urinated.

We were able to sober him up before he had to pick up "Miss Ann." When told what he had done, he was even more shocked than we had been. Narrowing his eyes and shaking his head, he said, "I will never take another drink of that stuff. It kilt me. Shuh! I was dead. I was dead! No more of that mess for me." That vow I think he kept.

A few years later, Buddy moved to Akron, Ohio, following the same path that so many black Southerners trod, moving directly North to industrial cities and establishing colonies of relatives and friends. For his part, Buddy took a job as a janitor at Sears, allowing him to buy my first bicycle at a nice discount. Dad taught me to ride it, a plain, no-frills "wheel," as he called bicycles. Later, when I got my Schwinn, a bike that I never wore out, Dad taught me how to take it apart, grease the parts and reassemble it.

As a factory laborer, he did not earn enough money to buy me a lot of toys, so he taught me how to make my own. There were the clothespin pistols that shot matches, striking them and propelling them aflame.

Pop guns were sold in stores, but Dad taught me to make my own by cutting a footlong piece of elderberry and hollowing out its pithy center. We'd whittle a plunger and use it to push a green piece of chinaberry fruit through the elderberry "barrel." The berry would explode out the end with a wonderful bang, traveling as far as one hundred feet.

How innocent those guns seem now when I think of young men today who, at the age I was then, get their first gun: an Uzi.

In a 1946 green Chevy Dad taught me to drive on the back roads outside Meridian.

But perhaps his most valuable teaching was done together

with Mother, through their own lives: how to live a champagne life on beer money, enjoying what is free in nature and appreciating what is valuable in people—humor, intelligence, kindness, willingness to work hard and play just as hard.

On my first job, it became clear to me that I was better at the playing part. At the Star theater, the "colored" movie house in the colored section of downtown, neighbored by the E.F. Young Jr. Hotel, Beale's Cafe and other black-owned businesses that, ironically, fell victim to integration, I got a summer job selling concessions—hot dogs, drinks, popcorn— in a huge box that I carried by a strap slung around my neck.

"Hot dogs, hot dogs, get your hot dogs," I whispered as I walked along the theater aisles, always keeping one eye on the screen, where a white cowboy hero was about to do in some bad red guys.

"Shhhhhhhhhhh!" always was the biggest response I got, as I never sold enough of the stuff to make it worth doing. Unless work for work's sake was the goal. I'm sure I never got any repeat sales; the dogs, by the time anybody bought any, were as cold as ice. And the iced drinks were as warm as the dogs should have been. Ever since those days, I've been skeptical of buying food from people who carry it around in boxes strapped to their bodies, even though I empathize with them.

In those old movies, now classics in black and white, the hero cowboy always was white. And in the Tarzan movies, the white hero always knew more about the jungle than the black servants. But none of this seemed terribly incongruous to any of us at the time. After all, in real life, we had the ultimate incongruity, segregation.

And, for most black people I knew, Jim Crow was angry-making but not crazy-making, something we cursed and survived until we got rid of it. My parents, friends and relatives used to rail against the system that not only denied us seats in white movie theaters but also shut us out of jobs that paid white wages. As I was nearing teenhood in the '50s, their anger, along with that of a nation, was swelling toward explosion.

For my part, I wondered what the "white" schools looked like, felt like, whether the water from the "white" fountains at the bus stations tasted better than that from the "colored" fountains. There were times when I seriously considered sitting at the front of the bus but dismissed the idea as about as ridiculous as sitting on a railroad track while a freight train bore down on me.

Knowing what lengths white people went to in order to avoid contact with me and other black people was puzzling at first, then humiliating, and by the time I was a teenager, it was infuriating. My way of dealing with this system was to treat white people with an inner contempt that matched the outer contempt with which they obviously held me. Dehumanizing them in the same way they had dehumanized me. This served to focus my anger and to develop a kind of pride that became both racial and personal. I liked myself as a black person and as an individual—regardless of what any white person thought.

For many years, far into adulthood, this attitude helped shape my behavior, making me a measured, contained person; giving my emotions to anyone—white or black—was an act that was far more deliberate than spontaneous. For a long time, there was no automatic trust or acceptance.

As my family anticipated the civil rights struggle, we also waged the continuing battle to keep food on the table. We went fishing all over the region, and I was in high school before I realized that we hauled ourselves off to lakes and streams because we had to eat, not because we were just having fun. Similarly, for years, I figured we gardened because we preferred home-grown vegetables, not because we couldn't afford the store-bought ones. And, for a while, I thought we listened to Blind Willie McTell and Big Mama Thornton and Robert Johnson and B.B. King and Muddy Waters and Billie Holiday sing about hard times and bad times simply because of their great voices, not realizing that parts of our lives were in their songs.

* * *

When fishing was just fun, it was really fun. All three of us had cane poles, about fourteen feet long. We'd stick them in the car, hooks, lines and sinkers dangling, and off we'd go. Among friends, exchanging intelligence on where the best bream or catfish could be caught was hugely topical.

Of the equipment we used, we bought only what we could not fashion ourselves. In addition to being economical, there was something satisfying about making fishing equipment: a float from an old cork, a sinker from bullet lead, canes cut from stands of bamboo. Satisfying in the same way that a homemade kite was. For people who were powerless in so many ways, this expression of self-sufficiency was powerfully intoxicating.

When we had found our perfect place (recommended by a family friend, declaring, "You can just about dip 'em out, there so many of 'em"), we would throw out our lines and watch the lead weight sink, momentarily tugging the cork underwater. The cork would bounce to the surface and then bob with breeze-blown ripples.

These times, sitting on a lake bank, watching a bamboo pole, when the only thing happening was the waiting, made for incredibly sane times. Sometime we would all silently enjoy the moment. At other times we would chat, as Dad spat tobacco juice or lit a Pall Mall. Mother would light one too, jutting it at an angle in her mouth, and squinting, to keep smoke out of her eyes. (My version of a cigarette in those days was rabbit tobacco leaves stripped from a wild weed and rolled in brown paper, smoked in private with boy buddies, certainly not around my parents.)

Sooner or later, the hit would come, disappearing the cork and pulling the line taut. Grab the pole, give it a jerk to set the hook. Maneuver the fish out of the water to either admiring looks or bemused glances.

No, we almost never threw any fish back, no matter how

Eddie Lee's first juke joint.

small. My parents would never have understood the sport of catching fish, weighing them and then tossing them back into the water in order to compete for a prize.

Back home, we'd (the royal We) clean the catch and fry them. The larger ones would get split; the tiny ones we'd fry whole, eyes, guts and all, and pop them into our mouths like shrimp. Add some onion bread, fried on top of the stove, fried potatoes, fried green tomatoes, and we had a meal fit for roy-alty. Add some blues, and we had it all.

> *Ummmmmm, Merry Christmas, Baby. You sure did*
> *treat me nice.*
> *Ummmmmm, Merry Christmas, Baby. You sure did*
> *treat me nice.*
> *Gave me a diamond ring for Christmas . . .*
> *Now I'm living in paradise.*

As a child, I knew the blues simply as music played around the house, not as an expression of the way life was. The Christmas season was not official in our home until we had played Charles Brown singing "Merry Christmas, Baby," with a sexy piano and church bells backing him up. After that, the cookies smelled real, the tree looked truly festive.

Over and over that song would play—an old record that would not have sounded right without scratches. Mother and Dad would latch on to each other and waltz around our tiny living room, singing as they went. "Merry Christmas, Baby. . . ."

The family listened to the blues not only at home; we'd shake our heads—and other parts—to the music in juke joints, too.

Going back and forth between Cuba and Meridian, we'd travel the old pre-interstate road, U.S. 11 and 80, which led us past Club Ala. Miss., a wide, green cinder block building that, during my childhood, was always a stopping off place for Mother and Dad.

It was my first of many juke joints, those crude, rude bars, dispensers of brews, blues, whiskey, fried sandwiches, companionship and more, those monuments to black Southerners' determination to have champagne fun on beer money.

I was about twelve when I was allowed to go in with my parents. Each of them would have a fish sandwich and a bottle of beer, while I shared the food and chugged a Nehi orange drink. Sawdust was on the floor, B.B. was on the jukebox, and danger was in the air.

Never did I go to a juke joint with my biological father, and I cannot imagine him in one. That is just one more difference between him and Dad. But while they never could have acknowledged it when all three of them were alive, my three parents had more in common than not — beginning with their essential dignity, their belief in earning their own way through the world and their insistence on treating people fairly and being treated the same way. Thus, together, they taught me more than they ever knew.

* * *

In some ways, the path to my reunion with my father was made smoother by my relationship with my stepfather. From the first time we met again, I had no recriminations against my biological father because, while I did not have him to grow me up, I had Milton, my Dad, as good a father as anyone could have.

As they taught me through example about living life in general, Mother and Dad taught me a specific lesson about living in public housing. Through their attitude and behavior they showed me that living in the projects did not mean, necessarily, living without dignity or without a garden. "I'm gonna have my flowers and my greens, I don't care where I live," Mother used to say. So, in our front yard of Frank Berry Courts, the two-story apartments snuggled next to a little stream we called "Diddley Branch" on Meridian's west side, we enjoyed the flowers—roses, gardenias, zinnias. And from the back yard, which, on a quiet day, was within the sound of the stream, came the vegetables that we ate.

It was around this time that we began calling the space where we grew vegetables the garden. But never did any of my three parents use the word garden to indicate a flower-growing spot. Fact is, neither my biological father nor Dad ever thought much of growing zinnias or azaleas or anything ornamental. That was Mother's work, which she did with gusto.

When the three of us moved out of public housing into a duplex, still on the west side of Meridian, we were in high cotton, as we had more space to spread out. We didn't have any more money, though. Thus, records and radio still were our chief home entertainment. Once in a while, we'd visit a neighbor who had a television set. But it had to be something special, like "Your Hit Parade" on Saturday night. After watching white, fresh-faced TV singers do the sanitized versions of gritty hits like "Work With Me Annie" and "Roll With Me Henry," we'd turn on R & B radio stations and hear the real thing. Stations like the one whose signal must have reached half of America, broadcasting out of Gallatin, Tennessee, with a show that I think was called "Randy's Record Shop." I never knew whether there was a Randy or a shop by that name. Or whether the name was a joke referring to the sex of rock and roll.

The move put us closer to Dad's brother Johnny, an Army veteran who spent time in Paris and dazzled me with French phrases, which he dropped into his everyday conversation for no apparent reason.

Uncle Johnny's pencil-thin moustache, much thinner than Dad's, was always trimmed just so, and it wiggled when he said something like, "Ooooh, la la," followed by a bit of tongue-clicking that recalled myriad B-movie detectives. He was a fop, but a charming one. And to a teenaged Mississippi boy, he was France.

How could I know then that this poor native son had fallen in love with a faraway place that treated him more like a man than he ever had been treated, and that he clung to these linguistic snapshots because he couldn't get the place out of his soul? He did not follow his heart back to Paris, as far as I know. The last we heard, he had got only as far as Indianapolis.

Our duplex (a preacher and his wife were our neighbors) also gave us space to grow more flowers and vegetables, and in our yard I had a sprawling mimosa to climb and harvest of its sweet blossoms. From those and from a million honeysuckle flowers, we neighborhood teenagers would suck nectar like grubby, giant bumblebees, falling drunk with pleasure.

But the South of the 1950s was no place to be idyllic. In August of 1955, when I was about to start high school, fourteen-year-old Emmett Till, a black boy my age, visiting Mississippi from Chicago, was kidnapped and murdered near Money, Mississippi. His offense: allegedly flirting with a white woman.

It could have been me. That was my first thought when I heard about the killing on the radio. And it wasn't like it happened in Georgia or South Carolina. But in my own state. That made the scariness even starker. And it made me even more conscious about not staring at white women. But it also intensified my anger at Jim Crow. I wanted to express it.

Others did too, of course. Fear and outrage rampaged through black communities across America. *Jet* magazine ran funeral pictures and showed Emmett Till's mutilated body. Before all the tomatoes were in, my parents were making plans to head north. Those preparations were accelerated by an incident at a little grocery store in our neighborhood.

I had gone to the store to buy a quarter's worth of candy, giving the white clerk a dollar bill. The young man rang up the sale, reached into the cash drawer and counted out my change. But instead of handing it to me, or laying it on the counter (a common custom in those days), he tossed it onto the counter, scattering the coins up and down the linoleum surface.

After gathering the change, I turned and picked out a pack of chewing gum, asked how much it cost, counted out the exact amount, flung it onto the counter, then stomped out of the store. Neither of us had spoken a word during the two change-tossings.

Later that day, I recounted the story to my parents with great indignity, relish and gloat, saying, "You shoulda seen his face when that money rolled all over the place!"

Neither Mother nor Dad said a word. Not to me, not to each other. Their only reaction was a look. By October, we had moved "up South" to East St. Louis, Illinois. Up South because it turned out to be like the real South in many ways, notably its economic deprivation and Southern-born population.

In preparation for the five-hundred-mile drive, we packed all our household possessions into a U-Haul trailer and a '50

Chevy. We also packed enough food to last us for at least twelve hours, as we, like all black people driving through the South, knew that stopping at a restaurant, even an inferior one, was likely to result in trouble, not food—unless there was a "Colored" window for take-outs. After so many years of Colored water fountains and Colored bathrooms and Colored schools and rides in the backs of buses, we just couldn't do one more Colored trip.

So, laden and looking forward to a wonderful new life up North, we struck out, on U.S. Highway 45, traveling overnight and hugging the eastern edge of Mississippi. Past Scooba. Macon. On past Columbus. Tupelo. Corinth. Then, boom, we were out of Mississippi, into Tennessee and feeling safer, somehow.

We flipped the trailer only once—in the middle of the night somewhere in Tennessee, spilling all our possessions and my spitz dog, Snowball, who was riding in the trailer. Somehow, we rounded up the furniture and Snowball, got back on our way and arrived with just about everything intact. However, for the next ten years we were reminded of the incident by a huge dent on top of the refrigerator. Snowball already had a dent in his forehead, the result of a collision with a car. Dad's mother had fixed him up by stuffing the wound with snuff. Healed.

We took our gardening ways with us, too. Surprising and disappointing, in East St. Louis, gardening for food became more necessary than ever. Dad, a seriously willing worker, seemed to be laid off from his job at a steel mill more than he wasn't. Often we lived on his unemployment check and Mother's tiny earnings at a laundry, supplemented by Dad's odd jobs. One of them was grasscutting in nearby Belleville, and he often would take me with him. We'd start at mid-morning, stopping for a lunch of sandwiches and cold drinks provided by the homemakers and delivered to us on the steps, where we'd sit and dine.

For many who got there earlier, East St. Louis, the gritty little town across the Mississippi River from St. Louis, was the mecca they had anticipated. Dad's brother Pete and his wife, Grace, were doing all right. He was still trading cars often, getting new ones like the red Ford he used to drive to Meridian when we lived there, demonstrating what riches were to be had up North.

To be sure, the East St. Louis of the 1950s had a swaggering energy. It was bad when bad was cool. Only half jokingly, folks would describe it as the place crooks came to when they were run out of Chicago. Crime and grime ran hand in hand.

It was the premier city of Southern Illinois, boyhood home to Miles Davis, home to Katherine Dunham and Donald F. McHenry. And by the late '50s, its population had reached more than eighty thousand. Factories hummed for those fortunate enough not to be laid off. And the railroads were so busy you couldn't drive across town without getting stopped at a railroad crossing—a sign of busyness, a signal that money was flowing like cargo on rail. So, like happy mice trying to find our way through a maze, we rushed from one intersection to another, trying to beat the trains. Roll on big trains; roll on with your moneymaking selves. *Look* magazine in 1959 named the town one of its "All America" cities for its good government and general progressiveness.

But by the 1980s, East St. Louis had become an all-American failure. Crime and grime remained, but not much money. The population had dropped by half since our arrival in the mid-'50s but ironically was no longer racially divided: The town had become virtually all black. Around forty percent of the town's households were receiving some sort of public assistance.

"The bottom fell out of that place," a Census Bureau official told me.

In the 1990s, East St. Louis joined a growing number of towns trying to bail themselves out of debt and despair through revenue from legalized gambling. Riverboat gambling, in the case of East St. Louis.

Of course we did not foresee any of that back in the '50s; we were there and would make the best of it, even with the frequent layoffs, even if it wasn't exactly what we thought it would be. At least we didn't hear of any black boys getting snatched and killed for flirting with white women.

This was the North, meaning that, for the first time, I could attend schools with whites. I did not. Given the choice of enrolling at integrated East St. Louis High, to which I'd have to ride, or to all-black Lincoln High, close enough to walk to, I quickly chose Lincoln, where I ran track and walked the two or so miles each way daily. Yes, the walking was good exercise. Not that we could have afforded to buy me transportation to get there.

No matter where we lived, walking always took me past somebody's house where, in warm weather, good R & B would jump through an open door. Fats Domino, the Coasters, the Silhouettes, Chuck Berry, Sam Cooke all sent me as I headed home, where I'd turn on the radio and listen to some more. Television still was rare entertainment for us in those days. But who needed it? On the radio, I could practically see ol' Chuck-a-luck duck-walking across the stage, never missing a lick on his guitar. "Sweet Little Sixteen . . ."

Of course, nothing could top any song that had my name in it: "Eddie, My Love" and "Mr. Lee" were the most notable.

And, just as white folks were listening to some black music, some of us black people were getting into Elvis and the Everly Brothers and "The Killer," Jerry Lee Lewis. At one point, one of my favorite shirts was a pink and black number like one that I'd heard was favored by Elvis.

As a former Mississippian ("Sip" to some superior-feeling East St. Louis boys), I was surprised to find an all-black school in Illinois, thinking segregation was a Southern thing. But, as it was explained to me, it wasn't forced segregation, like the Southern kind; it was simply that only black people lived near the school. Soooo . . .

At the same time, I was happy to discover that, like Harris High, my old school in Meridian, Lincoln offered crafts courses that at least got many youngsters interested in becoming bricklayers or carpenters. As it had been in Meridian, my selection was wood shop. But it was here that I got my first introduction to gang violence, albeit a relatively innocent kind.

One day, in my second semester, as I was putting the finishing polishes on a magazine rack in my woodworking class, a stocky boy of sixteen or seventeen skulked in, followed by several buddies. They stood, looking around the huge room, where saws buzzed and hammers pounded. One by one, the sounds stopped, all but my sanding.

The leader of the pack pimped over to me, shoulders rolling from side to side, eyes narrowed. I didn't know him, and as far as I knew, he didn't know me. He didn't introduce himself. In fact, he said nothing at all. Instead, he picked up a piece of wood and broke it on my ribs.

I looked around for somebody to hold me back. There was nobody. So, trying to sound more angry than shocked, I said, "What'd you do that for?"

"You don't like it, meet me on the football field after school," he said, turning to rock on off.

For the next several hours, I tried to figure what was the right thing to do. Go to the metal shop and make a weapon? Take a piece of wood and ambush him? Try to quickly form my own gang?

The last fight I had had was in Meridian with the girl next door when we were both about seven years old, a strange turn of events considering that, a year earlier, we were exploring each other's private parts behind my parents' sofa. Odd that we chose that spot, as it put us squarely in the window in the front of the house. In any case, that last fight with her was the only one I had ever won, and I attributed my victory to eating shredded wheat. Moreover, I never had been in the habit of fighting, any more than I had been in the habit of dancing, feeling that both were a waste of time and energy—energy better spent talking, or exploring.

Anyway, it was clear to me that should I fight this guy, it likely would be a losing battle, even if he didn't bring his boys. Nevertheless, honor would force me to at least show up on the football field. So I did.

I waited, no metal weapon, no reciprocal piece of wood. With a chill wind blowing and darkness approaching, I stood there long enough to satisfy my honor, then started the walk home.

This mysterious young man never started anything again, never mentioned the incident. Years after high school, I saw him on the street. He greeted me as if we were old friends.

What had it all meant? I didn't ask; he didn't tell.

None of my real friends, including my best buddy, Carol Ann, she of beautiful smile, sweet lips, wide wool skirt, tight sweater, thick bobby sox and long-lace saddle shoes, had ever heard that this was some kind of initiation rite. What I did know, however, was that if we had battled, there would have been no end to it except a bad one—perhaps a fatal one. Meaningless deaths were common in East St. Louis in those days, as they are today, everywhere.

While I was in high school, we still owned the little black '50 Chevy we had driven from Meridian. On many Sundays, our family entertainment would be to drive to 15th Street and Broadway, park the car and just watch people. We would have driven over to the airport in St. Louis, to watch the planes land and take off, as did some of our friends, but like many East St. Louisans, we rarely crossed the river; it might as well have been a thousand miles away.

Psychologically, it was. St. Louis, like Chicago, represented the alien part of city life in the North: too big, too fast, too impersonal. The "East Side," on the other hand, was slower, more comfortable, more familiar. More like the sleepy little towns so many of us had known "down home."

So we'd park on the street, or sometimes on a store lot. My parents would often bring along some beer to sip, while I'd drink soda and eat the remnants of popcorn I'd brought home from the movie (an all-black movie house, just like the one in Meridian). Similarly, this corner on Broadway was black-only, except for the Chinese people who owned the "chop suey joint."

Through our windows on our world, we'd watch the show—couples strolling, dressed for clubbing, knots of young men standing around watching women walk by, tossing out the obligatory, "Hey, baby! You looking good TO-DAY. Can I go with you?" Unlike today, there was an understanding between the men and the women that such comments were fun flirting, not serious hits. Therefore, most women would smile and say something like, "Not today, thanks," or, "Sure, come on," knowing that wasn't happening.

Those days are gone. While they weren't the most elegant way of relating, such exchanges in their own way represented a kind of acknowledgment and appreciation that men and women no longer express. Today both are afraid they will be misunderstood. This change is a low-level example of a more serious loss: men and women increasingly are afraid to flirt or engage one another, particularly strangers, on this level. As poet Maya Angelou points out so powerfully, romance is fading from our everyday lives. These days, we think that if we flirt or compliment, we have to go to bed. And, of course, we're afraid to do that. Too dangerous.

But in those times in that place, watching people and hearing their harmless flirtations provided wonderfully inexpensive entertainment. The kind we could afford.

Amazing though, how much of poverty's sting could be dulled by such outings, and by a good shot of blues, a bottle of beer and a fresh mess of greens grown in the garden. Not called "up South" for nothing, East St. Louis was filled with

Mother and Dad at home, 1958, pause before heading for church.

people like us who grew food proudly and ate it necessarily, having learned the art and craft down South. We gardened at most of our many residences in the gritty little town across the Mississippi River from St. Louis. (We lived in seven different places in our first three years, each time looking for something better to rent. My parents weren't shakers, but they certainly were movers.) When a residence had no ground, we borrowed space from friends, creating a kind of community garden.

When friends, neighbors and gardeners would meet perchance at the gardening spaces, they often would commiserate about the travails of life "up here," where all the good jobs seemed to have disappeared before they arrived, and they would reminisce about the friendliness and natural joys of living "down home," which grew more attractive with time and distance. This group of expatriate friends numbered about a dozen, including two of Mother's buddies, Bertha and Jessie, and Dad's pal, "Tootie Fruity," a tall, thin man with a penchant for saying, "Well, yeah."

They took solace in growing food and flowers and of course in eating the food, too. My family and our friends would fill holidays, any days, and one another with chicken, dumplings, dressing, green peas, stringbeans, or snapbeans as we called them, and enough pastries to open a bakery.

For entertainment, we'd sometimes play dominoes, slapping our "bones" down at the end of a game and demanding that the losers "count 'em up."

The kitchen in that old house should have foot-grooves in the floor from the time folks sat at the table, drinking Mother's "tequila" and praising the latest crop of peas or beans they had produced in the garden.

"Y'all outdone yourself this year," Tootie Fruity would say. "Pass them beans."

"Shoot, this ain't nothin'," came Mother's reply. "You shoulda seen how big and tender we grew 'em down home. Musta been the soil."

"Uh huh," said Dad, "musta been. We're going back home one day. You just can't grow food up here that tastes like it did down there. This is so good it makes you hurt yourself."

"Make me want to haul off and slap somebody," said Tootie Fruity.

Of course, for all their bragging about how wonderful life was down home, none of the expatriates, including Mother and Dad, ever left East St. Louis alive.

And many of us who did leave came back.

Leaving was a must for me. Perhaps I harbored some deep-seated realization that East St. Louis was no place to grow, or even to grow up. But where to go? Certainly not to college.

I graduated high enough in my high school class ranking to earn a scholarship to any university or college in Illinois. But what could college possibly teach me, I reasoned. So, in September 1958, I joined the Army instead, signing up at seventeen for a three-year stint as a child soldier.

But first, the prom. The highlight was not the girl; it was the car, a yellow 1957 Ford Fairlane convertible. It belonged to my cousin, Johnnie White, a Korean War vet, and it was about the only thing he had to show for the years he spent in the Army, including a hellish stint fighting. The only thing, unless you count the screwed-up stomach that Johnnie blamed on Korea.

A boyish-looking thirtysomething, he was passing through town around my prom time and volunteered to lend me the car "because, with this car, you can get as much trim as you want."

Well, at least I got a lot of attention that night. It was such a special night that I actually drove across the Eads Bridge to St. Louis, where we had breakfast at some incredibly chic hour after midnight, laughing that "Twilight Time" by the Platters was floating out of the jukebox.

Nobody was awake when I got home that night, but Johnnie probably had taken a quick look out of the second-story window, just to make sure the car was all in one piece. He never stayed in one place very long, crisscrossing the country in that car, then others after it. About ten years after my prom, we learned that he had died, after spending time in a VA hospital. Finally, he had stopped hurting from that Korea stomach problem.

The son of my mother's oldest sister, Johnnie and I had not known each other well, but from that prom night on, I loved what he stood for. Freedom. The power of his car—my car for a night—its openness and the sense that on that night I could do anything I wanted, be anywhere I wanted at any time, all combined to exhilarate. For the next three months, I reveled in that, as I sat on our tiny porch on Boismenue Avenue, waiting on September, watching the trains travel the raised track across the street, singing my favorite song that summer, "For Your Precious Love" by the Impressions, and reading books. *Mandingo*, by Kyle Onstott, Aldous Huxley's *Brave New World* and *After Many a Summer Dies the Swan* and Joseph Conrad's *Lord Jim*.

Many years passed before Mother and I sat in her kitchen, and she told me how desperately she wanted to talk me out of joining the Army, how as her only child, I was too precious to be put in jeopardy.

"I wanted to stop you from going," she told me later.

"Why didn't you?" I asked. "You could have; you had to sign for me."

"I just didn't," she said. We poured ourselves another scotch.

As it turned out, I volunteered at the best time possible: after Korea but before Vietnam. As I had decided that college couldn't teach me anything, I surely would have been drafted to become cannon fodder in 'Nam.

But none of us had a clue about Southeast Asia when I announced my decision to Mother and Dad; we only knew that I could be sent anywhere and told to fight anybody at any time. Nevertheless, Dad either drove me to all the places that I needed to be in order to do the deal or lent me the car to drive myself. To the recruiter, to the place for a physical in St. Louis. He even helped me figure out which little pills I needed to take in order to make sure a second examination would not show too much albumin in my blood, as had the first.

Finally, I was all done, accepted. And, while I read books and waited for my adventure to begin, the two of them went about their business as if all was OK, hoping it would be. And possibly, hoping that my big adventure really would be just that. After all, we all had heard that the Army'll not only let you see the world; it'll make a man out of you.

SOLDIER BOY

If weight were the measure of a man, I grew up fast, going from 145 pounds when I joined the Army at seventeen years old to 175 just sixteen weeks later. From my first days at Fort Leonard Wood, Missouri, where I survived eight weeks of basic training, I learned that the Army ran on potatoes, milk and meat.

And a college career started to look better all the time as I cradled a rifle and crawled on my belly with bullets whizzing overhead. Tear gas, hand grenades, M-1 rifles, machine guns, bazookas and handguns all became familiar allies during those first weeks. Not exactly designed to prepare me for a career, of course, but that would come later. First I, like all recruits, had to become a fighting man. Then, as later in Vietnam, black men were overrepresented. The Army was, for many, the best job America was offering. For many, the only job.

In a battery of tests, I had shown some aptitude for communications, according to the test evaluators. So I signed up to become a radio operator. Morse code. Dit-dah-dit-dit . . . dah-dah. If I ever decided to return to civilian life, that skill would be transferable, I reasoned. At least more so than firing an M-1.

I had been warned that the Army almost never gave recruits what they signed up for, just as it never used a person's civilian skills. Thus those who were cooks in civilian life became truck mechanics in the Army.

So I was pleasantly surprised to learn that in my second

GI Eddie, Ft. Riley, Kansas. Playing war games by day, bar games by night.

eight weeks of training—something called Advanced Infantry Training—I was to go to Fort Riley, Kansas. And I was going to be made a radio operator, just as I had been promised.

But instead of getting assigned to some fancy communications unit with powerful state-of-the art radios lining all the walls of a room, I was given a radio about the size of a back pack. In fact it was strapped to my back. In the war games we played, either the platoon leader or I would talk with other units, calling in "artillery strikes" or asking for "armor," tossing out jargon like, "Roger, Echo 6, that is affirmative. Over."

The radio was known officially as a PRC-10. Given that, during wars, those carrying this radio usually stayed at the front of a platoon with a second lieutenant, making a tempting target, complete with waving antenna, it is fitting that soldiers called this equipment the Prick-10.

My unit, the 1st Infantry Division, known as the Big Red One, was scheduled to go to Germany in early 1959. So from the time I arrived in Kansas in late 1958, I knew I was going to Europe. Ah, yes, this was what we all joined up for. See the world.

But if I were going to hit the shores of Europe as a seasoned GI, I had to get the really important training before leaving the States. So by day I played war games, and by night I played bar games. Manhattan and Junction City, Kansas, were the nearby towns, notable for their symbiotic relationship with the nearby base, as were hundreds of similar little towns across America. The liquor flowed; my taste ran to rum and Coke, and, naively, cognac and Coke. These were days when people loved GIs. Before Vietnam.

To be sure, the military uniform was a badge of honor in those days, and I did enjoy the pageantry of parades and the precision and rhythm of marching. On my first Christmas leave, I went back to East St. Louis wearing my dress greens decorated with a blue infantry cord, marksmanship medals and a few other doodads that came with the unit. This getup drew a whole lot of good looks, and I wore it proudly. My civilian buddies loved the outfit, and it drew admiring glances from girls. My parents were happy for my happiness and proud of my military pride. And mother loved the weight I'd picked up, satisfied that I was eating right.

Seeing the contrasting reception that Vietnam-era GIs got a decade later was a chilling thing. Timing is everything.

In such a time, without the pressures of being disparaged by protesters, it was easy for me to make the transition from civilian to soldier, to be thrown into the company of strange men after growing up an only child. They were my family, with whom I ate, slept and talked. We camped in woods, only remotely aware of how beautiful were the trees in fall and winter. And none of us complained that our barracks were plantless. My agrarian roots had taken a back seat to the headiness of soldiering. Before enlisting, I had not thought of how different life would be in a "home" with so many "brothers." Fortunately, it worked.

A few months after my triumphant return home, I was aboard a troop ship, along with 1,500 other GIs, on a nine-day cruise to Bremerhaven. I loved being able to stand on deck and see nothing but water in any direction, to feel and smell salty breezes that, as an inlander, I had never known.

Years later, those days came back to me in places like St. Simons Island, off Georgia, and Cape Ann, Massachusetts, where gusts from the sea gently rustled the lovely marsh grasses. Because I escaped seasickness during the cruise, I decided right then and there that I could have been a sailor. And because I later came to love the sea and the grasses so much, I decided I could have been a sea coast dweller. The older I get, the more strongly I feel that. It is as if the ancient pull of water that affects us all grows more intense with age. Or maybe it is the combination of calm, power and fury that appeals to me, the sea's ever-changing, yet constant presence.

On that voyage to Germany, when I got ticked off because I had to clean up somebody else's vomit or peel potatoes and scrub pots on kitchen police duty, I made myself think about how much worse off my ancestors from Africa had been on their journey across the Atlantic. The sea breezes and beauty had not been theirs to enjoy.

Instead of America's eastern seaboard as a destination, it was a relatively cheerful Bremerhaven for me. Welcome to Germany, GIs. No chains. At least none made of iron.

A train ride and truck ride later, we "fell out" onto the parade grounds at desolate Baumholder, known to thousands and thousands of ex-GIs as one of Germany's worst places to be stationed. It was a dump, not near any large town, a post so big that it essentially was the town.

Still carrying a Prick-10 in an infantry unit, I spent much of my Baumholder time on maneuvers, camping out in various woods, huddled in the cold, the wet, and finally the warm.

During frigid mornings, you could walk among the tents and the loudest sound you'd hear was the pop of "snapper caps," beer bottles with a spring top attached. POW! POW! POW! went one after another, as sleepy men crawled out of sleeping bags and chugged a little alcoholic warmth before lining up for gruel. Inevitably, somebody would pass around a bottle of cognac to sweeten our canteens of coffee. This was our Cold War.

At last came the late German summer, making maneuvers almost fun. We would take German marks to the boondocks, and when the inevitable young German boy would show up, we'd give him a few marks to buy us bread, cheese, salami and wine. Still, the most remarkable thing about that was that never, ever did a boy fail to return with the goods and the change.

One warm day (seventy-five degrees, maybe; I never saw true heat in Germany), after my unit had been camping out for almost two weeks—with no showers—it began to rain, a frog choker. Scrambling as if to go to war, all of us ran to our tents, threw off our clothes, grabbed bars of soap and ran back outside. There were hoots and howls all around, and, alas, no women. That was the first and last time I have ever showered in the rain, but I have threatened to many times, and never do I see a cloudburst without looking around for a bar of soap.

The warm season also brought with it people on streets of tiny towns, looking curiously as our convoys rumbled along their cobblestone roads. Still, it seemed, it was close enough to Double-U Double-U Two that American GIs were subjects of curiosity.

But no subjects were so curious as black soldiers.

My first encounter with my surprising exoticism came deep in the woods, in a little gasthaus, where I had gone alone at the end of a day to get some schnitzel and beer—partly because I had tired of the canned rations and partly because I was desperate to mingle with civilians and to learn something of the culture and language. They were called guest houses, but these places were more like pubs than inns.

"Schnitzel und bier, bitte," I ordered, having set a pattern that would last me a lifetime: in a new country, first learn how to order food and drink. The schnitzel was breaded just right, hot and tender, recalling Mississippi pork chops. And by this time I had come to appreciate Europe's uncold beer.

Coming up for air, I noticed several old men at a table across the room who couldn't take their eyes off me. Eventually, after I made contact with one and nodded, he motioned me to join the table. After they had treated me to a couple of schnapps, one got up enough nerve to do what he had been dying to do all evening. He touched my hand. Lightly and with the most remarkable concentration.

"Broun," he said softly, incredulous. "Broun. Nicht schwarz." He, like other Germans, had always believed that black people were really black. Black GIs who'd been in the country a while said Germans had gotten this misinformation, along with a few other myths, such as our growing tails, from white GIs. Nobody ever asked me about a tail, but seeing brown skin blew a few minds.

It was a fun night with the old men in the bar, an evening of learning all around. I got my first introduction to the image abroad of America as a crime-ridden, crook-infested country. Sometimes the image is the reality; that one has only grown more stark since those days. On that night, when asked where I was from in America, I replied, "Illinois." The immediate response was, "Chicago," followed by a burst of simulated machine-gun fire. During my two years in Germany, that scene was played again and again. It was fun for me then, like something from a '30s movie. Little did I know those days would come back for real, with people in Chicago and every-where else in America killing one another like dogs.

Later that year, a miracle happened; I received orders to report to radio school. I was getting out of the infantry and into Morse code, maybe later into a unit with the radio room lined with sophisticated equipment. For sure, I was getting out of Baumholder. School—some two months of listening all day long to Morse code, learning to translate the dots and dashes into letters of the alphabet at increasingly faster speeds—was in Bad Kreuznach, a real-sized town, with far fewer GIs than Baumholder. Great news.

Indeed, it was possible to walk down streets of Bad K, as we called the town, and see more Germans than American sol-diers. But, as in most of Germany in those days, it was rare to see any black civilians, other than American dependents.

One night I saw a young German shop girl, auburn-haired, about my age, eighteenish. She was looking for a bus, and I was looking for her. We talked and talked and promised to meet again, this time on purpose, to have a meal and more talk.

At the appointed time a couple of days later, we met at a restaurant, barely ate, barely stopped talking, babbling in English mostly, resorting to pantomime and the bit of German that I had learned, babbling in the way that two interested people do in a rush of something new.

We left the restaurant and began walking toward her bus stop, maybe a half mile from the restaurant. About halfway there, we passed a field whose tall grasses and weeds seemed to beckon through the darkness. We went there, slowly, neither of us saying a word, just holding hands, tighter, tighter. Once in the field, we held each other hard, kissed for a long time, then sank to the ground.

I had done what Emmett Till only implied. And I had lived.

On one level, this was a simple case of boy and girl being attracted to each other and making love. Moreover, she was white because practically all the girls in the town were white. But on another level it was much more. This was freedom. This was exploding the myths of inferiority spouted by every white racist in Mississippi. Now I understood why Europe had so attracted and intrigued black American men. Being accepted and loved—or lusted after—by white European women balanced, maybe even obliterated, the hate and rejection white Americans had thrown at us for so many years.

The girl and I never talked about any of this. Language barriers certainly were one reason. But even without them, it probably would have been impossible to build a conversation with all the layers of feelings and experiences that our encounter signified. Impossible because as a young German woman, she could never imagine what life was like for a young black man in the American South.

In any case, it seemed fitting that I should give her my Lincoln High School graduation ring. So, right then and there, I pulled off the gold band with the onyx setting and slipped it onto her finger, feeling in that moment that this was a long-term thing. It wasn't.

After I left Bad K a few weeks later, we never saw each

other again, despite our notes and cards that talked about where and when we'd get together. Still, I appreciated what she had meant to me, and I always hoped that, somehow, she knew.

Now a trained intermediate-speed radio operator, I was assigned to the communications section of an ambulance company on a base near Mainz. My most important duty there was pulling an eight-hour radio shift, usually midnight to 8 a.m., during which I made hourly communications checks by Morse code. Chatting with several other units, I essentially said, I'm receiving your signal fine, and everything's OK. Had the Soviets been attacking, I presume I would have been sending out warning signals and calling for help.

My commo hut was a far cry from that wall of radios I had envisioned, but, at the same time, my phonograph-sized radio was a long way from the Prick-10. And it was stationary. Between those hourly commo checks, I read. My interest was running to Jack Kerouac, Richard Wright, James Joyce and Colette. Wright's *Native Son* resonated greatly with me, while Joyce's *Ulysses* provided challenge by its sheer volume. I wanted to be on the road with Kerouac and in bed with Colette.

During these overnight radio watches, I also took my "box" and a few record albums. Feeling kinship to the Beat Generation, I turned on to jazz, buying a few albums, including Miles Davis's brilliant *Walkin'* and his lushly orchestrated *Sketches of Spain*, both recorded before he stopped playing cool jazz, my kind of jazz.

Among my five or so roommates was another jazz lover; his name was Graham, in his mid-twenties, a mechanic in the motor pool. Graham, also a Beat wannabe, was jaded to the bone and had the best collection of jazz I'd ever seen. He was deeply drawn to Dakota Staton and Frank Sinatra.

At the time Graham—GI's always called one another by last names, feeling, perhaps, that if a buddy was killed in war, the pain wouldn't be on a first-name basis—was, in my experience, unique. He was the first white person I'd met who seemed genuinely color-blind in the best sense of the expression. I don't recall ever talking about race with him. Never did he volunteer that some of his best friends were black, that he had dated black women, nothing. Is that the mark of a truly liberated person? I wondered. But how could he be truly oblivious to the issue that had defined relationships between whites and blacks throughout my childhood?

I decided he was all right. And that he was one of those refreshing people who'd rather do than talk about doing. For many of us, that attitude covers anything from working to loving to living with folks unlike ourselves. Don't just talk about doing right; do right.

We did everything we could to turn our room into a beatnik bar, drinking red wine by candlelight, with cool pieces from Miles or Dave Brubeck or Chris Connor floating on our pipe smoke. Our uniform of choice was civilian: dark bulky sweaters, dark pants, German shoes.

One Halloween afternoon, Graham and I were laid back on our bunks, smoking cigarettes, drinking wine, and talking. We had no music because my box was broken, and he had lent his to the Service Club for a Halloween party.

By about four o'clock, we decided we had made a mistake, that we ought to go to the club and take back the record-player, a folding machine about the size of a medium-size suitcase. So we walked the block or two to the orange-and-black decorated club and found the saddest sight we could have imagined: a room full of GIs playing "pin the tail on the donkey" and dunking for apples as Halloween-party music played on our box.

We had to take them out of this embarrassing misery, so we unplugged the box, folded it up and hurried out the door, accompanied by the pitiful sounds of grown men whining, "Hey, what are you doing?" "You're messing up our party."

"Bring that back." Back in the barracks, we had to open another bottle of wine to clear our heads.

While Graham and I were grooming ourselves for a life of decadence, another roommate, Washington, was preparing himself for the ministry. Like me, Washington was a black Southerner—he was from Mobile, Alabama, about the same age as Graham, who was from Pennsylvania, I think. We were all the same rank, Specialist Fourth Class, equivalent of corporal.

Washington had decided that he wanted to be a preaching man. I had always believed preachers were "called," usually in some dramatic way, like at midnight or while walking down lonely roads just before seeing a burning bush. But, no, Washington was actually preparing himself for the ministry by thinking about it and by living a life that was 180 degrees opposite Graham's and mine. Washington didn't drink, didn't smoke, didn't listen to our music, didn't go off to town looking for love.

While Washington and I were headed in vastly different directions in life, we were drawn to each other by our common history as Southern black men. Thus, we enjoyed talking from time to time, sharing notes on living—and surviving—the Southern Black Experience. Like me, he had never been to Europe, but he seemed less curious about it, instead anxious to get back to The World. But then, he had a plan for the future; I was cramming all I could into the present.

Thus, I made sure I used all my leave time for travel in Europe. Very early, I discovered Amsterdam, "The Dam," as GIs called that city of canals. My first of several trips there was memorable for the man I met on the train, the girl who buzzed me on the street and for the women I couldn't believe I was seeing in the windows.

Leaving Mainz, Germany, heading north to the Netherlands in the early spring of 1960, I was nineteen and as free as I had ever been. I was dressed in civvies that I had bought in

Wiesbaden, I had no one to report to—parent or officer—I was going to a place I'd never been and where I knew no one. And I could go into any public place without worry or fear. Damn. I could even sit at a lunch counter if I wanted to.

After the train had rumbled along for half an hour or so, one of the other passengers in my compartment, a man of about fifty, asked in Dutch-accented English if he could treat me to a drink. Sure, I said—cognac and Coke.

"Coke!?" the man said, genuinely offended and incredulous. Then, turning parental, he said, patiently, "You must never ruin a good cognac by drinking it with anything like that. If you must drink it with something, use a beer chaser."

Half his advice was superb; not since then have I ever mixed cognac with anything. Also, I have chased it with beer. In moderation that works OK. On this day, however, we were not moderate, arriving in Amsterdam totally blitzed.

Somehow, I got a cheap hotel room, got to sleep and awoke the next day refreshed and in love with the city, which appealed to me as much for its open innocence as for its decadence. The two seemed to blend in the window boxes of flowers: fresh flowers displayed in old, old containers that had survived so much over the years, even war. For me, this was a new way of seeing flowers. Window boxes instead of clay pots on East St. Louis porches and white-painted car tires in the yards of rural Alabama. I liked the change, partly because it was change, representing the new experiences I was soaking up like a dry sponge tossed into a bucket of water.

The universal spirit of joyful openness is embodied forever in the young girl (by then, sixteen was young) who, seeing me eating fried potatoes from a sheet of newspaper rolled into a cone, headed straight for me, jogging lightly down the sidewalk. When she got to me, she smiled, took two or three potato curls, smiled again, and skipped away.

Far from innocent were the women—"business girls"—who worked what was a kind of sex district. I knew how far I had traveled from Cuba, Alabama, when I saw women sitting in shop windows, offering sex for sale. Some used rear-view mirrors to look down the sidewalk, thus knowing when to preen for a potential customer strolling by. Of course, their lovemaking techniques were as mechanical as their mirrors. But hungry men were satisfied, after a fashion.

Back at the base in Germany, Washington couldn't believe his ears when I told him about my adventures in Holland. However, he did not rush to pack his bags for a trip there.

I could barely wait for my next leave, heading for Paris later in the spring. The songs had not lied to me; the city was enchanted, the flowers and gardens were marvels of nature and human creativity.

But all that could not compete with the awe I felt at actually being in a city whose air was so sexually charged. Maybe Uncle Johnny knew something, I thought. Women in cafes played parts that I later learned were stock stuff in movies. "Do you have a light, Monsieur?" It took me a while to learn that "Do you have a light, Monsieur" was not much about cigarettes.

Some people, of course, never do anything subtle. Not wanting to be misunderstood, some women hung around hotel entrances, grabbing at men's crotches as we walked by— long before Michael Jackson made infamous his own crotch-grab. I'd never been propositioned so openly. And if their methods were lacking in romantic mystery, they were undeniably direct and unambiguous, I reasoned. And, for a nineteen-year-old in a strange land, the certainty of a woman's feelings, or just behavior, is hugely happy-making.

Paris suited me. I was happy that I had gotten two weeks' leave to spend there, even if it did mean eating nothing but fried potatoes and frankfurters, with beer (the only food I knew how to order in French).

Water was not something I thought of during these meals. Then something happened that made me think of water for a very long time.

At the top of the Eiffel Tower one gorgeous sunny day, I stood looking down, imagining what the tiny people below might look like close up. From up there, they all looked the same, like ants.

"It is a beautiful view, isn't it?" The rhetorical question had come from a red-haired, tanned-brown woman of about thirty-five, elegant in pink, bold in what she implied with only a smile.

"Yes, very beautiful," I said.

"Would you like to have a mineral water?" she asked.

We sat, talked and sipped leisurely. That was my first mineral water. And my first married woman. She said that her husband was in New York on business, and therefore it would be best if we went to my hotel instead of her apartment. That day, for the first time, the crotch-grabbers were still as I entered the hotel.

For the rest of my two weeks, I enjoyed her company and got to see more of Paris than I ever would have without her. More important, I got to experience the beauty of a relationship with a grownup, someone who had experiences and experience and who assured me that life was good, to be enjoyed, not just gotten through, and that living it and loving it fully was the right thing to do. We ate at fun restaurants, enjoyed good wine. We even packed a picnic and drove to the country. We talked about the deep meaning of life, and about its absurdities as well. Perhaps our relationship rested on some of both.

The teenager in me could not believe I had seduced, been seduced by, a grown woman, a woman in her thirties. But the old soul in me knew it was a natural thing. I had never been ill at ease with women. Of any age. Quite the contrary. And I had always believed that they were beautiful at any age. Or could be. This time, then, was my true growing up, never mind my age. I felt wonderful. And I felt expectant, looking forward to more growing, more women. But I certainly did not feel through with this one.

As with the girl from Bad Kreuznach, my Paris woman and I exchanged letters but did not see each other again. Either my time or hers was always wrong. Her husband, my military leave—something got in the way enough times to make us stop trying. This time, however, it hurt a lot more. To make love, then leave, then promise to meet again, then not do it. Was this growing up, too?

How could I survive on an Army post, once I'd seen Paris and Amsterdam? Not well, without spending most of my free time off post, waiting for my next vacation. As I was interested in getting to know Europe, I didn't spend enough time on post, doing GI activities, to make friends outside my outfit. I had to go out there, off post.

During a shopping foray into nearby Wiesbaden, I ran into Washington, walking down the street.

"What the hell are you doing over here, Washington? I didn't think you ever left the barracks," I said, kiddingly. But, the truth is, always has been, people don't kid.

"Just looking around," he said.

We agreed to have dinner together at a nearby Italian restaurant. After stuffing ourselves with pasta and schnitzel, we ordered drinks. Cognac for me, Coke for Washington.

A few sips into the drinks, I said, "Washington, I thought you didn't drink."

"I don't," he said.

"Well, how come you're drinking that Coke that has cognac in it? You didn't know I told the waitress in German to put a lil 'yac in there."

"Ahhh, you didn't do that."

"Yes, I did."

What had started as Washington's total disbelief now became mere doubt. He was looking suspiciously at the glass, sniffing it. But he continued drinking from it.

By the time he had almost finished his drink, Washington

was transformed. Usually mild-mannered, he began hitting on the waitress. "Baby, you sure look good. Can I go home with you?"

The good-natured waitress, who probably had heard a lot worse, could not have known what a shocking departure from his norm Washington's behavior was.

We left the restaurant and found a bus back to base, with Washington hollering out the window as we passed women on the downtown street. "Hey, fraulein, hey," he'd bellow through the open window.

Washington was drunk. In fact, however, there was nothing but Coke in his glass.

Later it became apparent that Washington had embraced that mythical drink of cognac as a liberating force. He changed. Not long after that night, he bought himself a black beret, same as mine, began drinking wine and eating bread, cheese and salami from our lockers—and most significantly, asked me to show him around Amsterdam. We took a long weekend pass to the city, and he had a ball. For the rest of his tour of duty, we hung out together, then more alike than ever.

I never told him about the drink.

After Washington and Graham left my outfit to go back to the States, and presumably back to civilian life, I still had about a year left on my tour. Having decided that I really wasn't going to become a career soldier, I stopped shining my boots, grew what beard I could (I was exempt from inspections because of my overnight shifts) and got out of town as often as possible.

On my last leave to Amsterdam in the summer of 1960, I checked into a youth hostel, in whose dining room I sat one morning, drinking tea from a bowl, smoking a pipe and reading a book on Zen Buddhism. A group of four or five Germans, teens like me, joined my table, and we became fast friends. So fast, that they invited me to spend the remaining week of my vacation with them in their hometown, Schwelm, near Dusseldorf. After catching a few jazz players at Amsterdam's clubs, I caught a train for Schwelm, while my new friends hitchhiked. They were waiting for me at the station.

The invitation, and my acceptance, flowed naturally and easily, though this kind of intercultural visit was unique to all of us. Either their parents had been prepared, or they were as spontaneous as their children; I got no strange looks or questions when I showed up with my traveling bag. And, after breakfast of liverwurst, bread, butter, jam and coffee, at the home of one of the girls, Heidi, her parents went off to work without a moment's hesitation at leaving their lovely daughter home un-alone.

After staying with Heidi's family on my first visit, I stayed with others on subsequent trips, always finding them warm, curious and friendly. In this tiny German town, with ancient cobblestone streets and geraniums spilling red from window boxes, I was an eternity away from East St. Louis and Meridian and Cuba. But I learned much about America's universal appeal. Seeing something of your own, whether a country or a home, or a lover, through someone else's eyes can be amazingly instructive, heightening pleasure and appreciation.

Like so many Europeans, my young German friends loved jazz, spoke English and read American poetry and literature voraciously. Many a night we spent drinking red wine, spiced with cinnamon, listening to Ella Fitzgerald scat—her voice riffing like a trumpet—and reading the impassioned poetry of Langston Hughes, the Bard of Black America. Years later, back in East St. Louis, the scene seemed racially incongruous, but then, it was natural, the way people were—and are—supposed to get along.

The extreme pleasure my German friends got from Ella and Langston and Charlie Parker and from my descriptions of the Mississippi River all served to ease my disquiet at the prospect of leaving the continent that had, in some ways, seasoned me for life. Europe had been that perfect combination of teacher and lover; I had learned and enjoyed.

Like many GIs before me, particularly black GIs, I found Europe so hospitable a place, so unfraught with the urgencies of race, that as my two years of European duty ran down, I thought seriously of staying on.

I could get a job in Germany, maybe go to college, perhaps even go to Paris and open a restaurant, as one former GI had done, becoming famous in the city for his meals of collards, pork chops, cornbread and other soulful delicacies served with French wine. Having eaten at the restaurant, I had seen it packed with French people as well as American expatriates.

Like so many half-formed, unformed germs of plans rolling around youthful heads, mine went no place. During my last visit to Schwelm, in the autumn of 1960, we rode motor scooters, fell in the mud and, after cleaning up and warming up, held long candlelit talks about what America and the world might be like if this man, John F. Kennedy, were to win the November election. Then we said tearful goodbyes, knowing I would not visit again. Soon after, to our delight, Kennedy did win, and in the early days of Camelot, I came back to America, back to the South.

At swampy Fort Stewart, Georgia, in the spring of 1961 I was still a radio operator but also a "short-timer," with just six months left in the Army. It turned out to be a surprisingly active half year. Instead of cruising to discharge in September, I propelled myself with abandon, as if to catch up with the two years that had passed while I was away from the country. Partying was my vehicle.

There to help me were Sarge, a career soldier around forty years old, and Jackson, a native Georgian who was twentysomething, medium build and clean-cut. We were all in an engineer battalion—one which, fortunately, trained very little and certainly built no bridges, thus leaving us rested and ready for weekend passes.

Sarge was a South Carolina "geechee," a short, wiry man with dark smooth skin and close-cropped hair. His speech patterns recalled languages of West Africa, the Caribbean and the Deep South of America. As a war veteran, a Southerner who had traveled the world and seen and done much, Sarge undoubtedly had stories that I should have heard.

But as a nineteen-year-old hellbent on burning my wick at any end, I was most interested in the facts that Sarge owned a fast black-and-white '56 Plymouth and that he was always willing to put it on the road for miles in search of good times.

Similarly, Jackson owned what is still one of America's greatest cars, a '57 Chevy, brown two-door hardtop, V-8 engine. This car was made for running and chasing.

Each weekend, I would pile in the car with either Sarge or Jackson. If it was a Sarge weekend, we'd go to either Savannah or Charleston, where he had friends and relatives. On Jackson weekends, we'd usually head for the Augusta, Georgia, area, where he grew up.

The partying started as soon as we were off post. Often Jackson and I would carry along a bottle of cheap wine called Hurricane Red, drinking the sugary stuff from paper cups as we rocked and crooned along to sounds of Ike and Tina, Ray Charles, The Shirelles and dozens of other R & B singers. Truly, I was back in The World.

Sometimes we'd stop in at Jackson's relatives near Augusta, driving the Chevy into the yard where it'd wait for us to fortify ourselves with a good greasy meal before heading for a juke joint in time to catch the prime-time customers. Round midnight.

One joint out in the country was run by a beefy woman who wore a frown and a pearl-handled .38, keeping order with just one look. She stood at the entrance, checking out each person as we entered. We always had the feeling that she had X-ray technology or a metal detector stashed somewhere in the room. Otherwise, how did she know to pull somebody over to the side and relieve him of his piece—without even patting him down?

I don't think this place had a name, but its game was eat, drink and be wary. Fights were frequent, usually broken up by the pistol-toting manager, who also carried a billy club. The food was, of course, fried—usually fish and chicken. And the liquor ranged from moonshine to "sealed" whiskey, as the legal stuff was called.

By comparison, a weekend of hanging with Sarge was positively elegant.

No juke joints; whether in Savannah or Charleston, we'd always have our fun at a house—his relatives' or friend's. And never did we drink bad liquor, certainly not moonshine.

Moreover, the visits to both cities introduced me to the wonderful live oaks that I have loved ever since. Their limbs, giant arms, arched across the cities' streets and highways, dripping Spanish moss that always reminded me of old men's beards.

And, having spent two years in Germany, where the growing season was so brief, I marveled at the almost tropical nature of these Southern coastal towns, where you could just about throw anything green into the yard and have it sprout roots and branches before your very eyes.

But, as always, the South could be as sinister as it was lushly beautiful. The same quality that made its swamps alluring—the brooding waters, the dense shrubs and trees, the mysterious sounds—also made them eerie. As Sarge and I whizzed by these murky spots on our way to lost weekends, we could almost hear the moans of nearly dead black men, disappeared many years before. These thoughts lived in us, but we tried not to dwell on them. We had fun to get to.

I had come a long way from Europe. There were ghosts there, too, similar ones in some ways, vastly different, too. The moans in Germany echoed from the death camps where millions of Jews were slaughtered. Yet my own limited experiences among Nazi descendants had given me less to fear than racists in my own country. In both places, I knew hate and trouble could rise again at any time.

At the home of one of Sarge's Charleston friends, I discovered what it felt like to be the older man. At twenty, I was introduced to a beautiful sixteen-year-old girl with milk-chocolate skin, long slender legs and an apparent desire to lose her virginity.

Each time that Sarge and I went to Charleston, I'd make sure to visit her. We'd take Saturday drives and Sunday walks and evening meals. After several such weekends, we drove to a quiet place near the beach and began kissing. Neither of us knew then that we were supposed to be in a Chevy. The back seat of the Plymouth Fury did just fine.

Our tender fun continued through the summer. She loved my war stories from Europe, and I loved her dreams of success as a lawyer. I had done enough and lived long enough to have a little past, but I was not interested in thinking about a future.

What we were doing, of course, was what youngsters have done through the ages: making sex as if there were no tomorrow and no consequences. In our case the consequences did not include any unwanted pregnancies; we quit while we were ahead.

As for the tomorrows, there would be others for me, and for her. Sex can be a powerful substitute for love as well as its companion. And for a twenty-year-old soldier, a twenty-year-old anybody, sex is much easier to understand than love. And at that age, sex works to confirm desirability and give the illusion of adulthood. With age, love dominates. Or it should.

In the meantime, there was much big fun to be had. In Charleston and Savannah and Augusta on weekends and holidays, and back in the Fort Stewart neighborhood in between those times. Back there, Hinesville, a tiny GI town languishing in Savannah's shadow, was the prime place for weekday hanging out.

Like Baumholder, Germany, Hinesville had nothing cultural to make it memorable. No noteworthy museums, restaurants or art galleries. And that was just fine; those were the last places that Sarge, Jackson and I were looking for anyway.

What Jackson and I were looking for (apparently his years had gotten Sarge over this kind of hunting) and what we found were some of the best juke joints in Georgia. GI towns have always known how to give GIs what we wanted.

The joints, like those in most places throughout the South, started as bootleg houses, enhanced by gaming and dancing. I learned later that linguists have speculated that the word juke is a mispronunciation of joog, the Gullah word for unruly, and that they further speculate that the word's origin is from dzug, an African term for wicked.

Wicked, for sure. Wicked and wonderful, as far as we were concerned.

Together and separately my buddies and I spent many steamy nights at the Blue Moon in Hinesville, drinking concoctions that have killed swiftly, smoking and listening to hard-luck songs and harder-luck stories from women who always turned stunningly beautiful as the hour grew late.

"I couldn't sleep at all last night," a line from Bobby Lewis's huge 1961 hit, "Tossin' and Turnin,'" sometimes would be booming as we walked in the door. On the floor, just inside, there'd be a huge metal washtub, the kind we used to bathe in back in Cuba, Alabama. This one was, in effect, a giant punch bowl. And punch was what it did. The ingredients: Hurricane Red wine, beer, chunks of ice and, for seasoning, moonshine. Paper cups were politely offered to all who entered. We'd fill our cups from the cold, vapor-shrouded tub, find a spot in the smoky room and lean back like we owned the world. In a way, we did—as much of it as we could get at the time.

Of course, the truth was, we didn't own a thing. Life for young black men in Hinesville, and in East St. Louis, as well, was a lot like swimming in boots: it was tougher than it should have been, and there was a good chance you'd go under. But if you survived, you'd feel like a winner. I was feeling like a winner.

Because I never wanted to learn any but a slow dance—or "slow drag" as we called it (except for my fling with the twist in the early '60s)—it took something like the song "Daddy's Home" by Shep and the Limelites to get me on the floor. But dancing wasn't the thing, anyway; being there was it.

For us, juke joints were, of course, places to meet women. But they had, and still have, broader appeal. While often feeling a bit dangerous, they always have exuded comfort in an uncomfortable society, warmth in a chilly, sterile world and sounds that seduce. These shabby places always have been divinely decadent.

As the summer of '61 neared its end, so did my Army career; by September I was no longer a child soldier, but a child veteran. Twenty years old. With no savings, no job and no prospects. I felt great. And why not? I was a civilian at last.

A NEW-OLD LIFE

Knowing that I had plenty of time for working, I decided to play just a little bit longer before heading back to East St. Louis. So I collected my discharge papers, said goodbye to buddies and caught a bus to Savannah, where I checked into a YMCA.

After about a week of revelry with the friends I'd made during my stay at Fort Stewart, New York seemed like a good idea, for no special reason. Still wearing my khaki uniform, I headed for the highway to hitchhike up the coast, a nice chunk of separation pay in my pocket and Jack Kerouac in my head. I was on the road.

Those were the days. Drivers of every description stopped for me: truckers, men alone, women alone, families. Days that will never come again. Thirty years later, I wouldn't have hitched, and I wouldn't have picked me up.

But that was then. A trucker who was cranking out the country music—back then I called it "hillbilly" and hated it—on his radio gave me a meal and a wonderful primer on driver survival: flashing lights to warn of a state trooper, courtesy blinks to tell the four-wheelers it's safe to change lanes. Later, a family with seemingly little to share insisted on sharing anyway, apparently happy to do something for a man in uniform. Those were the days.

Once in New York, East St. Louis started to look real fine. I had seen the world. Now I wanted to be home. I missed Mother and Dad, the comfort of knowing how to get some-place without having to look at a street name. Not even the bright lights of the big city—even this one—could change that. So, after a day or so of sightseeing, I hit the road again, and again I got great rides. The last one, two men in their early twenties, took me all the way from Indianapolis to East St. Louis. Along the way, we shared snacks (theirs) and stories.

Grateful, I invited the two fellows into the house for showers and dinner. Not knowing when to expect me, Mother had to deal not only with the surprise of having a wandering son return but also the shock of accommodating two gritty strangers as well.

They were the first white people I'd ever seen take a meal in our home. They didn't know that, of course, and my parents didn't make a big deal of it. After a couple of hours, the two visitors were back on the road, heading west to Kansas City. Not knowing they had made family history in my house.

It's too sad that hitching got to be too dangerous; it was a great way to go for budget-conscious travelers. My trip from Savannah to New York to East St. Louis cost me less than twenty dollars, and I made better time than I would have on the train—just as my German friends had, hitchhiking from Amsterdam to Schwelm, while I rode the train.

There's nothing like going home again to discover how much you've changed. Three years earlier, I had paid little attention to places in Europe. After soldiering there, I greedily devoured mentions of Paris or Frankfurt or Amsterdam, taking opportunities to tell of my adventures there. But most friends listened with more politeness than curiosity. It was another world.

Also, I was struck by the racial division in my town. That was not new, of course. The city's residents had lived mostly segregated lives ever since we'd moved there, but that became more glaring because of my travels to places where racial issues seemed less than absorbing in ordinary social life.

In a sense, the Army and college offer at least one important experience to young people: they both put various ethnic groups together in everyday situations. Seeing someone of a different race padding to the shower with a towel wrapped around his body does tend to humanize that person.

How long I had been away was obvious in smaller ways, too. Finding a simple bottle of red wine—a bottle with a cork—took some doing. And forget about a loaf of unsliced bread.

But East St. Louis was home. I had come back. I would settle in.

The first step was to apply for unemployment money and look for a job. College still was an unattractive option for me.

As Mother and Dad gave me a place to stay, I drew enough unemployment compensation to keep me in decent clothes and, more important, to finance the monthly note on my first car, a blue and white 1956 Ford, V-8 engine, stick shift. Dad, seeing that I had fallen in love at first sight of the five-year-old automobile, helped me inspect it and cosigned.

It may be that a man's first car is a more significant passage than his first sex. A man's passion for a car is full-blown at a young age; it does not need years of driving experience to enhance it. But in a man's passion for a woman, experience in love and life adds dimension, makes passion fuller and more beautiful.

Maybe the passion for cars comes early and easily because the automobile puts us in control of where we can go, how quickly we can get there—no small concerns for a young man. (Similarly, I have always preferred stick shifts because I like to be in charge of when the transmission changes gear.) For some of us, certainly for me, it takes years to learn that a woman can be as liberating as a fast car.

In any case, I remember that old Ford far more vividly than I do my first lover. At age twenty, when I bought that car, I was already a skillful driver, but I still didn't know much about love.

That certainly didn't stop me from looking for it. Most of the places friends and I went were not as raunchy as the juke joints I'd known in Georgia, but they weren't ritzy, either. Two of my favorites—Midtown and Pudgy's—were simple taverns. You walk in, sit at the bar or at a table, and hope that some women alone will do the same thing. The music on the juke-box was much softer than juke joint fare, tending more toward Nancy Wilson than Memphis Slim. Many of my nights were spent searching places like this, while my days went to fruitless hunts for work.

Meanwhile, Mother and Dad bought the first home they ever owned together—brick, one-story, with a basement and an attic, on Hall Street. I turned the attic into a bachelor pad. After setting it up with a phonograph, bed, bureau and table, I covered an entire wall with photographs and postcards— mostly from friends I'd had in Europe and Savannah and Charleston.

At this time we were still corresponding—Karl and Heidi, my hitching friends from Schwelm, were in college in Germany—and I was still connected emotionally to them and to their towns. But like so many relationships held together by the glue from postage stamps, these gradually fell apart. For a while, my lover girl in Charleston and I talked about her taking a bus ride to visit, but it remained just talk.

I didn't want her visit to happen. I felt that it would intrude on my new-old life, and I knew that such a visit, in those days, would have indicated to her and to her family, if not to mine, that we were near marriage. And I was a long way from there.

The bachelor pad hummed with dates, who never seemed put off by the piles of beer cans, barbecue bones and wine bottles.

Perhaps searching for a natural counterpoint to this mess (my cleaning it up would have been too simple, and Mother wisely refused to even go up there), I began gardening indoors. But in keeping with the early '60s, everything had to have an edge, so I potted my pothos and Jerusalem cherry in quart beer bottles whose necks I had broken off. Drainage? Forget about it. Somehow they stayed alive for a year or so.

Whether this gardening, albeit strange, demonstrated the influence of genes or environment is unknowable. Probably it was a combination of both. Whatever, I have come to believe that gardening truly does represent order for me. It brings peace in a chaotic situation. That worked at my parents' home in East St. Louis, amid physical chaos of my own making. However, I was to learn later in life that gardening's salutary effect has limits. Time would teach me that gardening could not bring order to extreme emotional chaos, simply because I would be too unhappy to grow anything.

Maybe Chubby Checker's twisting shout stimulated (read that, scared) the plants into survival, or maybe Chris Connor's smoky voice soothed them, or maybe the attic's desert-hot temperatures kept them from root-rotting. In the winter, heat from the rest of the house rose, and in the summer it shot right through the roof from the white-hot Midwest skies.

All the better for gardening in the back yard, which my parents did, building a fruitful vegetable garden and a sensual flower garden at this home, while I worked my way through a series of jobs, including furniture salesman, insurance salesman, laborer and postal worker. Partying hearty those days, I gardened with my folks on some weekends and at night tried to avoid the jagged edges of the beer bottles.

The furniture sales job, which began as a stock clerk job at a discount store, got me off unemployment a month or so after I got it started. I never got back on.

As sales jobs go, it was definitely low-end, more like canvassing. I would drive into neighborhoods, knock on doors and make pitches for refrigerators, TVs, radios and phonographs.

"Good morning, Ma'am. My name is Eddie May. I'm here to share some of our bargains with you, if you could just take a look at these lovely brochures. Appliances of all kinds. Easy credit. Could I have just a few minutes of your time? I know you won't regret it. Thank you very much."

I was always surprised when someone would promise to visit the store, even more surprised when she'd buy something.

But my biggest surprise of all was that I could actually knock on a stranger's door and stand there without twitching nervously, as I had always seen myself as publicly shy, anything but a salesman. Fact is, that sales job, along with a couple of others, were the best preparation I could have gotten to be a journalist. Selling anything requires selling yourself, and to get information, you have to do the same thing.

Nowhere is that truer than in the sale of insurance, or 'shonce, as many East St. Louisans called it. Convincing people to buy something as intangible as life insurance is convincing them to buy you.

Squeezed in between selling furniture and insurance was perhaps the strangest job I've ever had—even stranger (and far more healthy) than my short stint stacking fertilizer bags at Swift.

It was a government job, of course, working at the Army depot in Granite City, Illinois, just north of East St. Louis, where earth-moving equipment the size of Texas was stored. When I showed up for work the first day, I felt absolutely lilliputian: rows and rows of giant praying mantises stood at attention, waiting on me and a fellow I'd known in high school, who also was just hired in this temporary job.

Albert Johnson and I were given a stash of very large plastic bags, which we used to cover the gargantuan tires on the earth diggers, tractors and other mysterious monstrous machines. One bag on each tire. To prevent dry rot, the boss told us.

Quick to discern the way the U.S. government worked,

Albert and I (who years later both wound up living in the nation's capital) covered maybe one tire every hour or so, then spent another hour or so "checking and evaluating" our work. The job appointment was up in 90 days, alas.

I've always wondered how long those covers stayed on. My guess is that a few weeks after we put them on, another couple of guys were hired to take them off. To prevent mildew.

Selling insurance did not provide me a lifelong career, but it did give me a lifelong friend, Edward Buchanan.

I was down on the ground, wrestling a set of brake shoes onto my car when I saw Buch's well-shined shoes approaching. "Hello, young man," he said in his best, deep voice (we later had contests on who could greet someone or answer the telephone in the deeper voice). "I have an opportunity for you."

He was recruiting insurance salesmen, or "debit managers" like himself for the Chicago Metropolitan Mutual Assurance Co. After listening to his spiel, I decided insurance sales would be better than furniture, so a few days later, I showed up in the company's St. Louis office and signed on, taking on accounts for about a hundred families who lived in East St. Louis. Buch had that many families and more as well, but we often would join forces and visit each other's clients, as the pair of us made an effective selling team.

"Hello, Mrs. Jones, I'd like you to meet my colleague, Mr. May. He's an expert on the kind of investment I've been talking about for you."

"How do you do, Mrs. Jones. Mr. Buchanan has told me all about your needs, and I have here a program that can satisfy them completely, and at a reasonable cost. Please look over this document, and feel free to ask any questions."

With that, Buch and I would sit back and look serious until it was time to offer the pen. "Would you like to pay one or two months' premium with this, Mrs. Jones?"

The two years were a study in excess, including huge meals, long nights of drinking and carousing galore. Some of the eating and drinking sessions wound up at Buch's home, severely testing the tolerance of his sweet wife, Marie, but giving their children endless stories for their old age.

My weight jumped from about 175 to more than two hundred pounds during my two-year insurance career, fueled by foods like the rib tip sandwiches that Buch and I would buy at a place on Kingshighway in St. Louis, then race each other down the expressway, across the bridge to East St. Louis, devouring the sandwiches before they were cold and chasing them with malt liquor. My face rounded, giving it that happy-face look that so benefits a salesman.

Buch, also about six feet tall, weighing more than two hundred, but given to walking lightly on tiptoes and sporting a genuine, infectious smile, already was around thirty years old and balding when I was turning twenty-one. But we were both boys in some ways, wearing those little narrow-legged pants popularized by the Beatles, strutting around in high-heeled shoes and driving dangerously.

Drag racing through the streets was regular sport for us, as he gunned his little Plymouth, trying to keep up with my Ford. Later I traded the Ford for a new 1963 Corvair, burgundy, stick shift, a car I adored and drove furiously. Obviously, Ralph Nader didn't care what I thought, though, as he called the car unsafe at any speed. Hell, any car can be unsafe at any speed, given a little bad luck.

Fast cars and even faster relationships seemed so natural then. Quantity was quality. But as I moved in and out of liaisons, I made an important discovery: I loved women. Not just made love with them. I loved them and wanted them as friends, lovers and darlings. I never preferred fishing or shooting pool with the guys (which I did from time to time) to talking or sharing breakfast with a woman.

I did not ask myself whether loving women could give way

to loving just one woman or whether it was better to be one way or another.

In some ways, this was a reflection of rudderless youth. I had no idea at the time, though, that I had so much in common with the president of the United States, whose bed exercises later became legendary. While my assignations were a by-product of youth, perhaps JFK's were a reflection of arrested development or an over-youthful self image. Nevertheless, he did become symbolic with everything young and hopeful in America.

All play and no work would have been anything but dull. But the insurance company would have paid me no commission. Or salary. So on many days Buch and I hit the streets humping, often lathering our faces with cologne or after-shave lotion following one of our elaborate lunches. We'd stick cigars in our mouths to squelch the smell of cognac and sometimes go out and collect as much as $500, $600, $800 from policyholders in a single day, particularly if it was around "Mother's Day," the day checks were delivered to welfare mothers.

These were monthly collections of weekly-premium insurance policies, once known as "burial policies," paying as little as $250 in the event of death—never enough to bury.

Collecting these premiums in person each month put me in at least one house in every East St. Louis neighborhood. Virtually all the policyholders were black. In some blocks I collected from as many as half the homes. My clients ranged from the most impoverished, with dirt yards and dirty children to the funeral home families and teachers and firemen who represented the town's upper crust. They were young, old, educated, unschooled.

All had at least one thing in common: they were extremely trusting. Most paid in cash—some as much as $100 a month—hard-got cash to be applied to what they viewed as a savings plan, paid into by many for twenty years. Realizing they could get a lot more life insurance for the same premium, Buch and I teamed up one summer and cashed in a lot of the old, weekly policies and replaced them with policies paid quarterly or annually.

Having done that made it a lot easier to enjoy visiting with policyowners, many of whom viewed us as family.

On hot days, they'd offer beer or lemonade, coffee during the cold. A quick plate of a special dish here and there—chitlins, barbecue, neckbones—helped me reach my two hundred-plus pounds. Loving women spread tables, and sometimes their wings, as the blues song says. Always hungry, I was grateful.

And, in some of the older people's homes, I saw some of the largest, lushest house plants I'd ever known. At one home in particular, Mrs. Bradley's, there was a tableful of unusually large African violets that made a striking display as you entered her front door. On a living room table she was growing violets in everything from clay pots to tin buckets.

Mrs. Bradley's display taught me a simple lesson, one that guided me to my own tableful of African violets years later: if you want big violets, put them in big containers. Forget that potbound stuff; violets have spirits too, and they want to be free. And at the same time, they, like most people, seem to love living in groups. Mrs. Bradley knew that.

She showed me also, just as my parents had, that you can grow beautiful plants without spending a lot of money. I have seen many a gardener growing prize ornamentals and food crops by collecting manure from horse stables and relying primarily on inexpensive seeds and cuttings instead of buying more costly plants.

A good garden comes as much from the soul as it does from the pocketbook.

MAN OF LETTERS

My memory of the end of my insurance career centers on November 22, 1963. Buch and I were having a meeting in a little building we were leasing for our fledgling insurance brokerage business.

We turned on the radio and like so many other Americans were stunned to learn that John F. Kennedy had been shot in Dallas. After a lot of switching from station to station, listening to the frantic reports that all told the same horrible story, we fixed ourselves long, tall glasses of gin and tonic, sipped, sat in a long silence, said a few words and headed to our respective homes. Everybody we knew—parents, friends, relatives—everybody, was in shock; it was our first assassination.

The dream that was Camelot had been shot down, forcing us all to reassess our views of reality, our expectations for a new country built on elegance and equality and prosperity for all. To some degree, I had been living a work life that also was built on dreams, having gone from one unreal job to another: the Army, sales, sales again, along with a few odd ones thrown in. I was only in my early twenties, but I was getting tired of aimless wandering through workplaces. If I had not yet settled on a career, I at least wanted the stability of a traditional job.

My hard, fast life in the insurance game had worn me out. I needed a rest. So I left Buch where he had been when he found me and headed for the post office, where I got hired as a clerk.

Of the men I'd known my age, most had done one of three things: joined the military, sold insurance or worked in the post office. With my new job, I had done all three.

In the mid- to late-'60s, when I worked at the post office, black people were just beginning to get postal jobs in large numbers. And in many towns, certainly in East St. Louis, such jobs had, for many years, been considered big-time, or at least middle class, like teaching and social work. As so many of us were getting into the post office at one time, we diluted the specialness of clerking jobs. In fact, at around that time, all three occupations seemed to plummet in status, not to be replaced by any comparable status jobs for the ordinary, college-educated black person. Another era gone by. And unlamented as long as we aspire to bigger jobs with greater status. And get them.

When I got mine at the post office, my parents stuck their chests out, knowing that I was in high cotton, perhaps set for life. What job could top this?

I got a lot of congratulations, but what I didn't get was a restful place to work. The job was untaxing enough—put letters in a case of pigeon holes, distributing them by state and city, take the letters out and tie them up when the pigeonholes are full, put more letters in.

So sorting mail was no heavy lifting (although we occasionally had to drag loaded sacks around), but socializing was what wore us out. The East St. Louis post office gave new meaning to the expression social work; the place was called Peyton Place. That was no exaggeration. Discovering who was dating whom was the biggest sport in the sprawling warehouse-like building on 20th Street.

Lovers who were casing mail fifteen yards apart had perfected eye signals that told each other they needed to meet in the break room to have a private chat. And like elementary school playgrounds, there was a lot of "She likes you," and "Did you hear that he's her stuff now?"

People have always gotten together in the workplace, of course, as they find one another convenient and are intimate on some level, however superficial, simply because they spend so much time together.

But the post office social scene was especially intense, I suspect, because the work there was more boring, or mindless, than work in most places. You could carry on a flirtation and never miss a work beat because mental concentration was virtually unnecessary. Yes, you did have to actually notice whether you put a letter in the right hole, and, yes, sometimes clerks (most of whom were quite conscientious) didn't, and yes, that's why mail to California sometimes wound up in New York. But when that happened, who knew who screwed up? And mistakes in the P.O. are not like those in an O.R. Thus, postal employees should be low-stress. So why do so many seem to shoot up the places? Bored to anger, perhaps.

To relieve boredom and make the hours pass, we would play "poker" by using street numbers on mail to find the best "hand" in, say, five minutes of casing letters: 2121 Center Street, for example, is two pair, and 3133 Appleton Road is three of a kind.

That was OK for a while, but the Game of Love was the big one.

Actually, it was the Game of Lust. "Wanna stop and get one after work?" was often how it started, "one" being several drinks. Sometimes I'd go with a group of men, other times we'd mix, thus making it necessary to get straight beforehand who was going to leave with whom.

Because postal employees worked shifts around the clock—mine were always at night, starting at 4 p.m. or 6 p.m. and sometimes running twelve hours—we never cared what time we stopped to get one. Often that would be six or seven in the morning, meaning the place at which we stopped was likely to be the East St. Louis version of a juke joint.

An enduring memory for me of my P.O. days is stumbling

out of a joint on Missouri Avenue at ten in the morning and seeing another man weaving along the sidewalk, holding a chicken bone up to shield his eyes from the sun.

Not only did we party after work; we could do amazing things with our thirty-minute lunch periods. Darryl Robinson, a postal buddy, and I would clock out, dash to one of our cars, race to a restaurant and order sandwiches, then go next door for a quart of beer and back to the restaurant for the food, dash back to the P.O., where we'd sit in the car or on the curb to kill the food and beer and light up cigarettes in time to get back on the clock.

Thirty minutes. Amazing how difficult it became for me to even eat lunch in such a short time when, on later jobs, I no longer had to obey a time clock.

Work and pleasure got complicated when a new employee and I started having lunch together.

When she and several other women were hired, there was the usual round of guesses about who was going to wind up as whose stuff.

I liked her from the start, her warmth, acerbic wit, self-assurance and tidy figure. Chats turned into meals and more. Soon we were a thing for our coworkers to talk about.

We had fun, but I had a back-of-the-mind problem with the notion of settling down with a woman who already had a young son. Passion persisted, however, and we got married in 1966, doomed from the beginning, as passion can take you just so far.

In a marriage that you don't believe will work, it is easy to find reasons for its not working. Such was my situation. I married, but I did not commit, as I was still married to the wild life that I called freedom. Freedom to hang out with my P.O. buddies and to, essentially, be a single man.

Going into what folks used to call a "ready-made family" is more and more common, and more and more likely the older we get. But, like marriage itself, relating to a stepchild is something we cannot be taught. It is something to be felt. Truly, that relationship is part of the package; had I been committed to marriage then, I would have been a better parent to my wife's son. But unlike Dad, I had not found commitment. So there were no fishing trips, no eager plans to teach a boy to drive a stick shift car.

In short, I wasn't ready. Maybe she wasn't either. In any case, talking often ended in hollering. And we lived in anger much of the time, no way to be married. Especially no way to be married and working at the same place.

We did have some good married times, and some memorable ones. Among them is the time we distributed telephone books to earn a little money above the mortgage on the single-wide trailer home we'd bought. As mind-numbing as the post office was, and as beyond mind-numbing as this chore was, somehow it felt solid and uniting, as if we really were a team, a family in the old-fashioned sense of pulling together in order to make ends meet.

Then driving home one day, I had my first experience with a pregnant woman in a car, the one every expectant father knows, that stop-the-car-I-feel-sick request.

I stopped in a hurry. It was my MGB, the last car I ever loved. It was always just washed; I sure didn't want used pizza splashed all over it.

We started off on a strange note, that MGB and me.

Red body and removable top, with black leather interior and chrome wire wheels, the 1965 "B" was sleek and seductive, my dream car. I bought it off the showroom floor and drove it around until about 6 p.m., when it was time to hit the clock at the P.O.

During lunchtime, I paraded my buddies outside to admire my new machine and spun one friend around to one of our sandwich places, top off, summer night air rushing about our faces.

When I got off work at 2:30 in the morning, I turned the ignition key, only to hear that old familiar unn-unn-unn, followed by no throaty purr. I couldn't believe it. After trying to start my brand-new car for a half hour or so, I did the unthinkable: had a mail truck push me to start the thing.

Yes, of course, I should have left it and had the car dealer pick it up the next day. But, noooo. The push did get it started. It also jammed the tailpipe into the muffler, turning the new throaty purr into a raggedy roar.

I loved the car anyway, despite its premature rattle, and despite its penchant for refusing to start whenever the temperature dipped below fifty degrees.

And despite its being a cop magnet. Once, around midnight, I had slowed down to cross the railroad tracks around the then-alive stockyards just north of East St. Louis, when a policeman darted out of the tall grass, red light frantically flashing atop his black and white cruiser.

The officer waddled over to my topless car and during the next five or ten minutes checked every car-related document I had. To his dismay, all my papers were in order. His voice falling, he said as he returned my driver license, "It's a good thing you got up off it when you did; you was fixin' t' speed."

Musta been the bashed muffler. In any case, this car was the right one for a twentysomething like me, who smoked black cigarettes with gold tips and kept cognac glasses in the glove compartment. I always joked that the dealer should have provided a shield to protect me from all the women who wanted to jump in and ride.

Mother loved the car, too, always getting a kick from roaring up to the laundry where she worked and unfolding her short but considerable frame to get out, greeting her co-workers jauntily. Dad, on the other hand, always eyed the MGB suspiciously, as it was not made in Detroit. What a pair our two cars made: the tiny sports car parked next to

Dad's huge white and gray Chrysler New Yorker, whose ash tray was labeled "ash receiver."

In some ways that contrast became a metaphor for our generational differences in the 1960s. By 1967, I had taken a liking to at least some parts of the hippie movement, grooving to music like "Light My Fire" by the Doors and "Whiter Shade of Pale" by Procol Harum, working up to Jimi and groups like Iron Butterfly.

Mother and Dad couldn't understand how I could still love B.B. and Muddy and also listen to that stuff. Nor could they understand how I could wear those weird flowered pants and beads around my neck.

One day I drove by to see Mother and Dad, walked along the side of the house and rang the doorbell, only to have Mother eye me suspiciously from behind curtains, refusing to come to the door for a very long time. Turns out she didn't recognize me because I hadn't had a haircut in about a year, and during that time, she'd seen me only in hats or caps. She was cool, though, trying to use that as leverage to get me into a barber's chair. No way; it was the '60s.

And no way were my new wife and I going to keep that little MGB with one child already and another on the way; we traded it for a Pontiac in 1967, the year our daughter was born.

So, ostensibly I had become a real family man: a wife, two children, a family-sized car parked next to a trailer in the 'burbs.

Certainly my relationship with my parents had gone through a transition. I did not see them very often. And when I visited, it was as adult as much as son. When I sat at the kitchen table, I could have a glass of tequila or a beer or two and lament with the best of them about low wages and the high cost of living.

My biological father was never mentioned as I grew into this world, and he almost never entered my mind.

I had hoped that having a child would make marriage better. That was unrealistic. In time I knew we weren't going to find happiness, and commitment was out of the question.

But what I didn't know then (and didn't learn consciously for many years) was that I had a barometer that never failed as an indicator of my level of contentment at home. Gardening was the gauge. If I was happy, I gardened. If I was not, I didn't—at least, I didn't garden well or with any great passion.

At our trailer home, the level was pretty low. We grew a few plants indoors—pothos, dumb cane—and outdoors I sort of grew grass, which baked in the treeless lot.

Meanwhile, life at the post office went on. One day, as Robinson and I were casing mail next to each other, he talked about how much he was liking life as a student at Southern Illinois University's new campus in nearby Edwardsville. At twenty-six, I still had misgivings about college but decided to go with Robinson to a spring festival at SIU.

Something about the campus, carved out of rolling countryside, felt right, so I enrolled for a couple of courses—logic and art appreciation—beginning in the summer of 1967. I was hooked. However, I never regretted waiting so long to start college; most things happen when they're supposed to. By then I was as ready for college as I was unready for marriage.

Thanks to the unchallenging work at the P.O., I could work at least forty hours a week and carry a full load of college courses, too. So happy to find this smorgasbord of learning and stimulation, I didn't even mind the daily sixty-mile commute: drive from home to class in the morning, drive back to the P.O. in time for work in the afternoon, work until midnight or 2:30 a.m., drive home and start all over again the next morning.

Surprising myself, I was committed to college; I loved being an older student, an Army veteran (particularly as I had served before Vietnam), and someone who actually had been to many of the places we talked about in world history courses.

While walking across the campus on April 4, 1968, I heard about a murder that certainly would be part of future history courses: the shooting of Martin Luther King, Jr., in Memphis.

Again there was shock. And for many years after that, I would see pictures of John and Martin on walls of countless living rooms across America, symbols of shredded hopes and punctured dreams. At least some people held onto the symbols.

Kennedy's murder was horrible and dispiriting, but King's seemed even more personal to me because his life's work had been focused so specifically on goals I believed in: racial equality, integration, color-blindness. To have him shot down by a white man sadly emphasized the difficulty—maybe the impossibility—of getting the country and its people to King's mountaintop. As a black man, as an American man, I felt bad for my country, cynical about its future.

At the same time, I grew more and more committed to college. But less committed than ever to marriage. Having finally found that higher learning was OK, I wanted the rest of my life to fit in with it, to make as much sense. Marriage felt confining, antithetical to the free feeling and promise for a fine future that I got from college. Like a giant key, college unlocked life's doors, and, in rapid succession, changes tumbled out. I left the trailer and moved back in with my parents, truly believing that breaking up our family was the only way to save each of us as individuals. Surely stopping the arguments would count for something. For one thing, it would make the house a less tense place for the children.

Soon after we separated, I quit the post office and almost immediately moved to Ohio, seeking a new start in the new decade. Fortunately, I was able to maintain some semblance of a relationship with my daughter—aside from child support payments—by virtue of her visits with my parents, who doted on her to no end and whom she has always remembered fondly. Tall and thin, resembling my mother in face if not body, she grew into a "little Riller" with a passion for life, while her brother, my stepson, grew into a fine young man who never seemed to blame me for my not teaching him how to fish and drive a stick-shift car.

CLEVELAND

Moving to Cleveland in winter could be called a baptism of ice.

I have always been convinced that the reason many Clevelanders were so cheerless was the weather. Just as many Californians seem unrelentingly cheerful, mirroring the ubiquitous sunny, warm weather, a lot of Clevelanders stared icily at their newspapers on buses, reflecting the fear that, at any moment in almost any month, you could get snowed on.

Fortunately, however, there were warm friends to be made there.

Stopping over in nearby Akron before settling in Cleveland, I stayed briefly with my first cousin, Henry Reed, and his wife, Liz. At times their marital stability made a part of me wish to know what such a feeling was like, but their ease and cheer and my resignation got me over this longing.

Akron had been the stopping place for several of Mother's brothers, most of whom got jobs in the booming rubber industry. Working at Sears, Uncle Buddy was the exception. Unfortunately, by the time I got to Ohio, he had left us, so I never got to tease him, as an adult, about what Mother's tequila made him do in our front yard in Meridian.

Buddy's and Mother's other brothers' migration was like that of so many other black Southerners. It was as if they got into cars in whatever state they lived in and drove straight north, stopping just after Kentucky. We went to Illinois from Mississippi; Mother's brothers went to Ohio from Alabama. A lot of new New Yorkers I knew had come up from the Carolinas.

And like so many moves I've made in life, I had gotten to Ohio sideways, from Illinois.

After a little hiatus in Akron, I headed for Cleveland, moving in with Uncle Jake, another of Mother's brothers, seeking a new start and a new job, living on my lump-sum post office retirement money.

Unk, a tall, lean man with twinkling eyes, a ready sense of humor and a mouth always pursed as if ready to whistle, welcomed me into his home like a father.

When other relatives learned that I was going to live with him and his wife, who he called Miss Annie, they told me this story: When Unk met Miss Annie in Alabama back in the '40s, Unk was in his thirties, and Miss Annie was in her sixties. She was relatively well off, having some $5,000 at her disposal, in property and savings. Unk courted and married her, believing that in not too many years he would be widowed and well off. They moved to Cleveland, where Unk went to work for the railroad.

Well, when I arrived in Cleveland some thirty years later, Unk was retired from the railroad, but he had come home to a full-time job, taking care of Miss Annie, who was mostly bedridden with afflictions of the aged.

Her wrath, however, was in full bloom, bursting out in screams to Unk to bring her a banana or see about dinner or bring her a drink of her favorite, blackberry julep, a sugary wine that Unk stocked in the basement by the case.

Through it all, I never saw Unk flinch. Nor did I ever hear him speak an unkind word about Miss Annie, even when she verbally boxed him about the head and shoulders. My initial pity for Unk's plight turned into admiration for his determination to do right even if fate seemed to have done him wrong.

He may have taken solace in outside company, but I never knew about it. I did see him fondly caress his dream car, a black Cadillac from the '60s, one with fins, one of the last I could distinguish from a Chevy.

Unk and Miss Annie, of course, lived on Cleveland's East Side. It was explained to me that black people in those days did not live on the West Side. Even visiting across the Cuyahoga River was bad for black people's health, I was advised.

Disbelieving that, I went to see a friend on the West Side in 1971 and, returning home, stopped for gasoline. The attendant at the service station approached my car, and when I looked up to tell him what I wanted, I stared into the face of a silver automatic pistol. The white man holding the weapon said nothing, but I got the message and the hell out of there. Later I tried to figure it: had a black man just robbed him? Did he think I was about to? Had he just robbed the station, himself? Nah. I got the message; I became a believer, visiting the West Side only one other time during my two years as a Clevelander.

While I was so frightened and angered that I would have been perfectly happy to see this man set upon by large policemen and jailed until he returned to his senses, the incident did not make me bitter toward all white people. Over the years, as I heard how such incidents were repeated in cities all over the country, I had the sinking feeling that racial violence and lower-level distrust and disharmony were America's permanent curse.

My incident made me wonder about all those black people from the North who used to visit us in the South and ask how we could tolerate the awful racial climate down there. Some of them had come from Cleveland.

Nonetheless, I was in Cleveland to stay. At least for a while. Back on the East Side, settled in my upstairs room at Unk's house, I began poring over the two daily newspapers, the *Cleveland Press* and the *Cleveland Plain Dealer*, looking for work.

Answering an ad one snowy day, I put on my blue suit and black Bally loafers, trudged to the Cedar Avenue bus stop and rode downtown to the IBM office, where I got the biggest surprise since I'd arrived: I was hired as an accounts receivable clerk.

Knowing the reputation that IBM had for conformity, I had shaved off my beard, and I made sure I wore a white shirt, diagonal-striped tie and dark socks. Unfortunately, the trek through Cleveland's salted snow that day ruined the Bally shoes.

But that was a small price to pay for a job at Big Blue. After wearing denim and khaki in the dusty post office, I was impressed at the notion of wearing a suit and tie to work. Also, wearing suits during the work week made me look forward to changing into my green bell-bottoms with yellow flowers on the weekend.

Life was falling into place. At around the same time I started at IBM, I found an apartment on 96th Street, near Cleveland Clinic, third floor of a four-floor walkup. And, finally high on higher education, I enrolled at Cleveland State University, majoring in English literature. And knowing it would be an easy A, I studied German, recalling my conversations overseas and confirming that my Army experience was good for something. By day I collected IBM's money for computer cards, and by night I collected credit hours at Cleveland State.

Fortunately, the apartment was quiet enough for me to read the millions of nineteenth-century novels I lugged around. And the residents were fun, including a young man who was an aspiring opera singer, a waitress who displayed her vibrator next to her living room lamp, and two beautiful sisters who wore short haircuts and drove a hot Camaro that always made me want to ride.

I knew life was better because I was gardening again. In my apartment living room I constructed a plant stand of cinder blocks and placed on it philodendron, African violets and epicia. Scattered around the floor were cacti, dumb cane, avocado and a pothos that wound some twenty feet around the windows and up to the ceiling. I still am amazed at how much pothos you can grow in so little soil.

* * *

Once I learned to stay "in my place," I began to enjoy what Cleveland had to offer. A great symphony and art museum, an energetic theater community. A Cleveland kind of juke joint that I used to pass on the bus on the way to work around eight in the morning. The door would be open in the summer, and I could see men lined up at the bar, drinking boilermakers of Stroh's beer and whisky.

At night, they went harder core, downing 151-proof rum without blinking. Why not just open up your stomach and throw in a lighted match, I wondered after taking a hit one night. Whatever they might have been doing to themselves (weren't we all, in some way), these men (rarely did I see women in this bar) seemed grounded in reality in a way that most of my white-collar colleagues could only imagine. Most did menial jobs, and all had pithy observations about the big issues of the day.

"They didn't have no business shootin' them kids over there at Kent," one would say. "Kids wasn't hurtin' nobody."

"Hell, naw," said another. "They oughta be shootin' them folks breakin' in folks' houses. That's who they oughta be shootin'."

The city's ethnic mixture (on the East Side) meant that I could buy real Polish food that recalled something of Europe. A Puerto Rican friend taught me to fix a dish with salt cod, tomatoes, avocados and onions, all sauteed together. And, for a black American culinary experience, there was the barbecued pig feet that I discovered at a little joint on Central Avenue. And the fried fish at a restaurant on Cedar.

My life in Cleveland was a metaphor for the way many black people live daily in two worlds. During work hours, I was one of just three black people in an entire department at IBM, while during off hours, I moved in and out of both white and black worlds, depending on the company I kept and the entertainment I sought. I have always seen that duality as an advantage, likening it to speaking more than one language. It has always kept my comfort level high when I am "the only one."

Conversations about these two worlds can be funny.

After I had been at IBM for about six months, a white salesman named Rick stopped by my desk after a big weekend to talk about his adventures on the East Side. Seems he had gone to a club around 105th and Euclid, where he was in the minority, bigtime.

"It was really cool," Rick said, excited by the memory. "There were a lot of cool-looking dukes there."

"Dukes?" I said.

"Yeah," he said, "and there was this one duke wearing this long red jacket. Really sharp."

"Duke, duke. Oh, you mean DUDE."

"Yeah. Right. Dude."

Relating can be tough, racially or linguistically. It can be especially tough when the twain meet.

Rick's point about the duke's long red jacket was lost in his effort to communicate, but it illustrates the sadness of fashion in those days. The jacket was a popular one, often something with tails reaching below the knees, usually made of polyester, and preferably in bright colors or huge checks. Amazing that Americans ever survived the 1970s clothing styles.

I can't believe some of the stuff I wore, aside from the green and yellow-flowered pants, which were a kind of hippie holdover thing.

But the red polyester suits and the crazy-patterned shirts with collars that stabbed me in the chin every time I turned my head—hard to know why I wasn't busted by the fashion police.

Actually, I did get reined in once. By a German shepherd soon after I adopted him and tried keeping him in my apartment. I adopted him for good reason: I was burgled twice.

The first thief stole several LPs and my new stereo, about the only thing portable. The building's maintenance man caught the second thief in the act and chased him down Euclid, making him drop two suitcases full of clothes, along with a typewriter.

In each case, what the thief got, or almost got, was nothing compared to the invasion of my psyche, the attack on my emotions. There is no excuse for breaking and entering somebody's home.

So I got the dog to make sure that burglar No. 3 would stop and think before kicking in the door.

The dog turned out to be pretty destructive himself. One day I came home from IBM to find he had gnawed huge chunks out of my mattress. A few days later, he had done in the box springs. Then the beast turned to the cheap chest of drawers.

But it was when he chewed the high heels off my mauve-and bone-colored suede shoes that I knew he had to go. I realized later that the dog was just trying to save my style life, knowing I shouldn't be walking around Cleveland or any other town in those shoes.

Of course, I wore them only when I was away from IBM. There, I was mostly corporate, although I did have fun wearing pastel shirts, thus breaking the unwritten all-white shirts rule.

Soon after that, I grew back my beard. As the only bearded one in the office, I knew the risk. Out of uniform. I sensed that my peers were more concerned than bosses that I was "breaking the rules." Unfortunately, in offices that is often the case; the higher-ups have more to worry about. In any case, I defused the issue for peers and bosses by announcing to a small group that I was growing a beard because I was reading for a play. I kept it for the next year and a half, with nobody questioning my original reason. During that time, the play *Hair* came to town, but surely nobody thought . . .

* * *

At IBM, talking was mostly what I did, as my job was to telephone corporate customers and get them to pay for the stuff they had bought. The list of companies ranged from the largest, highly computerized manufacturers, banks and hospitals to small occasional purchasers of cards.

One day, while having one of our frequent conversations, an accounts payable woman at one of the smaller companies and I turned our talk to after-work activities.

"So, what are you going to do after work?" I asked.

"I don't know for sure," she said. "I'm thinking about stopping for a drink."

"Sounds good to me," I said. "I could use one, myself. Crazy day."

"Yeah. Want to join me?"

"Sure."

"OK, I'll pick you up in front of your building. Tell me what time."

"Five-thirty."

"Great. I'll be the redhead, double parked in the yellow convertible VW Bug. Just walk over and introduce yourself, and I'll move over so you can drive."

Sure enough, at the appointed time, I walked out of the office at 777 Rockwell and saw the VW Bug double parked, a red-haired woman in the driver's seat. "Hello," I said, "I'm Eddie."

I thought she'd had a heart attack. She fell back and stammered, "You, you are?" Momentarily, she recovered, however, and moved across the stick shift into the passenger seat. I slid in and drove us to a nearby bar, where we had a drink and she confirmed my suspicion: during our many telephone conversations, she had assumed I was white.

But she was OK during our brief chat, afterwards driving me to my apartment, where we quickly said goodnight. As fate would have it, I inadvertently left a glove in her car, which she mailed to me. We never saw each other again.

That date remains a sardonic memory for me. I chuckled about it in the same way black people often recall racial affronts. Laughing to keep from crying. I was embarrassed for her, and at the same time I resented her embarrassment and her inability to overcome it. Here was another hurtful example of the race problem.

The incident also helped me understand why so many black people sometimes signal their race over the telephone, saying something like, "I'm a third-generation Spelman graduate," just in case a white person on the other end of the line speaks too freely. Doing this saves the black person from getting angry and the white person from getting embarrassed. Very light-skinned black people who are mistaken for white have similar problems in groups of white people where racist comments get tossed around. They, too, often send signals that they are black.

Preventing people of any group from bad-mouthing other groups in private would be a futile quest. However, you'd think that, after all these years and all these embarrassments, people would stop assuming it's all right to make disparaging public comments about people of different races. But no group is even close to that point.

Several times when I talked with IBM employees at the data-processing card plant in Greencastle, Indiana, they would marvel at my living in such a dangerous city as Cleveland. In a typical comment, one said, "I don't know how you do it, with all those coloreds running wild."

I was tempted to say, "You know, I'm black," but I never did. However, I eventually did tour the plant as part of my education about how the company worked. "Hi, I'm Eddie," I said to each of my telephone colleagues, smiling faintly on the outside and howling with laughter inside.

They were not amused, probably suffering from the peculiar habit of feeling tricked even though no trick was played, blaming someone else for an embarrassing assumption.

* * *

In the office, I had several face-to-face friends, including a woman named Sylvia, young, heavyset and filled with biting wit. Another was Jackie—older, thinner, worldly. For reasons I never knew, they did not get along at all.

Also, I didn't know that by having lunch with Jackie, I had offended Sylvia. In one of the stranger episodes I'd seen in a workplace, Sylvia stopped speaking to me for six months after she saw Jackie and me returning to the office from lunch. It was my most vivid experience to date with the no-talk treatment, something I learned was not uncommon among sad little people who have no better way of communicating their anger or helplessness.

The problem with this tactic is that many people who use it don't understand that something so drastic cannot be undone. At least, not for me. Sylvia later apparently decided she wanted to resume speaking. That didn't work for me, as it simply recalled the foolishness of stopping in the first place, thus further alienating me from her.

Knowing this about myself, I have never tried to punish a friend or lover or spouse by withholding conversation, something so basic and necessary to human interaction. Taking it away, I always knew, would do permanent damage to a relationship.

As office friendships go, Mike and I had one of the best at IBM. He also became my all-time best example of someone suffering from low self-esteem.

A young man just back from Vietnam, he took a low-level job at IBM, where his father had worked for years, and bought a motorcycle, a big one, big enough for two. He even bought an extra helmet, which he kept fastened to the bike. Problem was, he said he could never get a woman to ride.

I really felt for him. One day we went to lunch at a square near the office, one with greenery, a fountain and more women than we could look at during a lunch hour. Like so many situations where men and women gather, the two sexes segregated themselves—in much the same way so many people of different races segregate themselves in colleges, demonstrating they have failed to learn togetherness.

"You say you want a date, Mike. Look at all these women, sitting around by themselves," I said as we headed back to the office.

"None of 'em would go for me," he said. "They never do."

"Oh, come on, man. Don't be like that. You gotta give it a try. All you have to do is just walk over to any woman out here and introduce yourself. I bet that by next week, you'll have some woman wearing that other helmet."

Mike seemed to be getting it. He smiled a little, put a little glide in his stride.

Just at that moment, I heard a tiny plop. I turned in time to see Mike raising his fist toward a pigeon streaking across the sky, as he shouted: "Go ahead, dammit! Everybody else does!"

Toward the end of my time as an IBMer, I met one more woman, at a building near my office. Having seen her in the lobby of the building, I introduced myself. We talked. She was a graduate student, nearing the end of her program.

By the time we met, I had become so cynical about marriage that I had advocated renewable marriage vows in a persuasive rhetoric class, and my favorite book was Thomas Hardy's *Jude the Obscure*, in which marriage led to "tragic sadness."

We all hope for good change, however, and I believed I had found it in this smart young woman. A native Southerner, she had an appealing clarity about her regional roots, as well as an admirable certainty about wanting to do the right thing to improve society. We had fun getting to know each other, and after a few months it became apparent that marriage was a real possibility. It was real despite warning signals that I could hear faintly, including my continuing love for the single life and my sense that she saw my daughter from my first marriage as some sort of competition with our current life. I remembered similar feelings from my first marriage.

But these were only whispers, easily drowned out by the belief that such minor differences would be wiped out by time. Early in relationships, most people do not try to change their partners. Nor do the partners worry about the prospect that they will be asked to change basic beliefs or behavior. Such was the case with us.

Thus, in early 1971, we ignored the whispers and got married.

For my part, it had become clear that I was not going to make a career at IBM, wearing pastel shirts as a way of flouting the company's conservative dress code. Studying English literature had confirmed my love for writing, and some form of communication seemed far more interesting than wearing yellow shirts.

How would I act on that love and earn enough money to live on as well?

Write novels?

Teach?

Work at a newspaper? Yes.

We learned of an internship program at the afternoon daily Cleveland Press, and I applied, winning a spot and shucking my IBM uniform in favor of ink-stained wretchedness. And there was still a college degree to get.

So, while finishing up my last year or so at Cleveland State, I worked at the *Press*, sometimes on an overnight shift, beginning at 11 p.m. Alone at the city desk, I'd make sure the wire machines were loaded with paper, organize stories for editors arriving early in the morning and man the phones, taking pathetic telephone calls from people whose only break from loneliness seemed to be reaching out to radio talk show hosts and, when the radio lines were jammed, to late-night newspaper people like me.

After a while, I stopped counting the number of people who called to ask the paper for help in eliminating radio signals that were being broadcast to them through tiny receivers implanted in their bodies by sinister forces.

Out of self-defense, I devised a solution for them—and me. Whenever I'd get one of those calls I would listen patiently and then advise the victim to place a one-inch strip of aluminum foil around his head, thus short-circuiting the evil broadcasts.

Every time I've gone back to Cleveland since those times, I've expected to see someone on the street wearing a shiny band around his head. And, fielding so many calls from lonely, confused people has prevented me from even thinking about working as a host on talk radio, especially late at night.

My internship turned into a reporting job, but by graduation time in 1972 I had decided to go to graduate school, sweating out applications at several schools, including Kent State, then notorious as an antiwar protester killing ground, Cornell and Columbia—the only graduate school I really wanted to get into. Unable to afford the tuition, I was thrilled when, on the telephone, an official thumbed through my financial statement and said, admiringly, "You're a financial basket case."

I was in, getting a fellowship that paid tuition and university-run housing that, for New York, was positively inexpensive.

My class was mostly white but had a healthy percentage of black students, a representation far better than the one in the journalism profession itself. The number of minorities in journalism never has been commensurate with our numbers in the population. But back in the early 1970s, we were barely present at all in many newspapers and television stations.

In some ways, this was the best of times for minority journalists, as we were so few that white journalists did not yet fear that we were taking jobs from them. Thus, minority journalists didn't have to defend our talent against charges of being "affirmative-action hires," a situation that materialized in the 1980s when more African-American, Latino and Asian journalists joined the profession. When I first noticed this backlash (white women, of course, also have been targets), I was offended, feeling it was an affront to those of us who brought talent and hard-won skills to our jobs.

Over the years it became clear to me—and to angry white men as well, I hope—that minorities may be hired because of color, but if they don't perform well they should be fired despite their color. True, many are kept on, but that happens with incompetent people of all races. Eventually, these arguments became less and less important to me. I became content to simply work hard and let the results speak for themselves.

HARLEM SOJOURN

My wife and I U-Hauled from Cleveland to New York in the summer of 1972, arriving on a Sunday to begin what was a solid year of both getting to know the city as subway-riding residents and enjoying touristy activities like going to the top of the Empire State Building and taking boat tours around the island.

To be sure, my year at Columbia's Graduate School of Journalism (known fondly as the J school and even more fondly as a trade school in Harlem) was much like a vacation. After working full-time and going to college during my entire undergraduate career, I felt positively idle, having only to go to school.

It was here that I dropped my first name, Eddie. The shorter, crisper Lee May seemed better as a byline. Ever since then, whenever I heard anyone call me Eddie I didn't have to look to know it was someone I'd known before 1972. My new name has confused some folks, though. Years later, I met a woman who told me she had seen my name on newspaper stories for several years and had pictured me as a Chinese woman.

My classmates could not have known that my ease and comfort with class assignments stemmed not from brilliance but from the incredible luxury of not having to go to work later. Therefore, they marvelled that I took leisurely lunches at the West End pub near campus with a classmate, Richard Harewood, who also had a history of working while in school.

Richard and I enjoyed hanging out at the dark, heavily wooded pub on Broadway, having beers and talks for hours, then, near deadline for a class-writing assignment, walking back to campus, to the old manual typewriters, shooting our cuffs and knocking out our stories while some of our fellow students pecked out a paragraph, then ripped the paper from the typewriter, balled it up and shoved another sheet in.

They thought it was life; we knew it was school.

But like life, school was fun, filled with discovery and introductions to people with whom I have remained in touch. You know it couldn't be bad. It was in New York City, and I was there when it felt livable, manageable.

Aside from these attributes, Columbia was worth attending just to see CBS legend Fred Friendly in action, the first journalist I'd heard warn reporters against pouncing on people whose relatives have just died in a flaming plane crash or a tornado, staring them in the eyes and asking how they feel about their pain and tragedy, maybe even hoping to make them cry.

Unfortunately, there have not been enough such warnings throughout the profession, and not enough heed paid to Friendly's disdain for the "How do you feel?" question.

Having always disliked invading people's grief in the name of journalism, I was surprised to learn that some don't mind, even relishing such an interview. Several times I have walked up to people whose relatives just got killed, expecting them to be too broken up to talk—only to have them actually start the conversation. Maybe they feel some release in talking about their tragedy. I hope that's what it is. But nothing can make me understand why people bare their souls and much more on television's tabloid talk shows.

Our apartment was real New York: small, windows looking out on buildings so close that they shut out practically all light and gardening opportunities. But the beauty of living in student housing is, in addition to the fact the price is right, you know it's all temporary.

Nevertheless, there were lasting lessons. One is, there's nothing like living in a place to get to know it. Even a place that is depicted in print and film as much as New York is. After riding in elevators, cabs, buses and subways with a zillion New Yorkers, I couldn't be persuaded that New Yorkers were cold, unfeeling and uncaring—despite what I'd been told. I'd seen New York men giving up seats on buses to old women, people actually talking in elevators and hurried executives pausing to offer directions to lost visitors. No sterile descriptives for New York, then. Loud, maybe. Insular, perhaps. Arrogant, yes. But what city wouldn't be if it offered you anything you want at any time of day or night? What a place to live if you're very rich.

But if you were poor, the contrast could make you crazy. And in New York I saw a lot of craziness: people who were poor in ways I had never seen in Meridian or in East St. Louis. While my poor family could grow our own food and catch our own meals from lakes and streams, poor people in New York more likely got theirs from the postman who brought their government checks. Maybe the lack of self-sufficiency, the lack of control over their lives helps make poor people crazy, drives them to the streets where they beg for money and seem not to mind having people step over them.

I could never envision my parents losing their dignity to that extent, no matter how little money they had. Obviously I did not feel a part of New York's rich world of limos and midtown condos, but I certainly did not feel part of the crazy poor world either. And seeing its awfulness made me certain that I never would.

Just as the stark differences between rich and poor were burnt into my memory, so was something I learned in the drug store at 110th and Broadway one night when I went to buy envelopes. At the checkout counter I noticed my wallet was missing. Dashing back to the aisle where I had seen a man who was dirty, ragged and furtive, I confronted him, demanding to know if he had picked my pocket.

No, he said, over and over. Unsatisfied but resigned, I left, walking the few doors around the corner to my apartment. Where I found my wallet on a table. Ah, Prejudice, thou hast a thousand faces.

My most important lesson was a twentysomething anthropology student. We met at the West End during lunch as she pored over papers from a graduate course and I fondled my lead paragraph for a story due in a reporting and writing class.

She was lovely in body and spirit, and fun to know and talk with. We drank wine and walked in the sunshine and watched the Hudson roll alongside Riverside Drive. We got to know each other well enough to seriously contemplate going overseas together, where she was to do field work for her doctorate and I would have written fascinating stories.

But in the end, I knew I couldn't do that. Just married for the second time, I felt obligated to do right, to give marriage a chance. She went. I stayed. I felt true and moral and upstanding, but I also felt like a fool. For the first time, I cried when I said goodbye to a woman. In time I knew I had done wrong. There are times when you really ought to follow your heart.

By graduation time in the spring of 1973, my wife and I had decided to move to Atlanta. It was back to our native South. We were like many black people who had lived up North but never lost touch with life down home. Like Mother and Dad, who talked about "going home" the whole time they lived in East St. Louis, I felt a pull to the region, its passionate excesses, its warm climate and people. Atlanta, of course, was the most magnetic of all, known throughout the nation as the "black Mecca" because of its friendly racial climate, permanent black middle class and economic opportunities for all.

I knew that no city could possibly live up to Atlanta's public relations billing. But I also believed that it was a good place to be. Any place known as the city of trees had to be pretty good.

That decision made, we spent early summer sending out resumes and having our final touristy New York fling before returning to the South.

CHASING DREAMS

Living in Atlanta in 1973 was a long way from living in Meridian in the 1950s. Time and struggle had fatally wounded Jim Crow, and, happily, it was apparent even to the hardest of the hardcore segs that the fall of segregation did not take the region down with it.

Since Mother, Dad and I left Meridian in 1955, the only time I had spent in the South was a few brief visits back home and my insular, good-timing trips to Savannah and Charleston. Living in the region again triggered vague thoughts about making a trip to Meridian to see my father, but they remained vague. I was close, two states east, but oh, so far away.

This really was the New South. I was not prepared for the sight of black men escorting white women to movie theaters or Maynard Jackson running to become to first black mayor of Atlanta or black workers munching next to white ones at lunch counters or black children and white children studying in the same classrooms. Aspects of King's dream coming alive.

My appreciation of such developments no doubt contrasted with the anger and fear that some white people felt, maybe still feel. But the more dominant attitude of Southerners seemed one that said, this is the law; let's obey it. Just as white Southerners upheld segregation when it was the law, most were just as conscientious about supporting integration when it became law. Whether that reflected some kind of regional do-rightness or just a desire to get on with life is debatable. The result was what counted.

* * *

I understood why so many people loved Atlanta. It had energy and determination, mixed with easy efficiency that made the city work without seeming to try too hard. We quickly got into that spirit, finding jobs, a place to live and hope for the future.

As a copy editor at the *Atlanta Journal*, my job of reading stories for errors and style, then writing headlines for them was far less interesting than getting to know the people who sat around the horseshoe-shaped desk with me.

The slot man, who sat in the middle and distributed stories to us rim people, was a longtime newspaperman who made writing important heads look easy and writing unimportant ones look like fun. He also was a wonderful creature of habit, making a regular afternoon telephone call to his wife at home that went something like:

"Hello. Yeah. Chicken pot pie. OK, bye." All meal discussions should be so easy.

Then there was one rim man, a quiet, gentle soul who was downright passionate about growing gloxinias. He grew them extremely well. Years later, I wished I had learned more from him about these often-difficult plants. He often talked elliptically, starting a conversation with, "Did you get yours?" It got your attention. As did his prized plants when he'd bring one in to give away.

Another rim man had a great hobby: collecting kitsch. He'd tell stories of scouring the countryside in search of another chenille bedspread or finding a great fake plant. He was fond of the ones with brown rubber stems and leaves of multicolored feathers.

He talked about having a party once, inviting some people who did not know of his kitsch collection. With great relish, he recalled how, one by one, guests would be shown to a room containing much of the collection—cheap little-boy fountain with water coming through his wee wee, black velvet paintings, the works.

Not knowing they were being put on, the guests would approach this shrine to bad taste and gulp, not knowing what to say, fearing that if they told the truth they would offend their host, who was no doubt busting a gut inside. "Ummm, how, ah, interesting."

That description fits the first apartment that my wife and I moved into. The complex looked great from the outside. Brick. Grass cut. Inside was OK, too, except for one problem. Well, two actually.

Roaches. Like I'd never seen them before, not even in my low-rent Cleveland apartment, which I thought had world-class insects. This was the first time I'd seen roaches living in a stove. Spraying, both professional and amateur, didn't even faze them.

This was an apartment of surprising superlatives. In addition to having the most roaches, we had upstairs neighbors, two men, who were the noisiest neighbors I'd ever known. Not only did they play their music at maximum volume, they'd trip the turntable arm so the same record would play over and over and over . . . then leave home.

Often, they'd both dress up in day-glow skirts of green or red or orange, along with matching pumps, and stand out on Donnelly Avenue, hollering at men in passing cars.

After a few months, we left the roaches and the skirted men for a tamer place. Once again, as in Cleveland, I had a place to garden. Indoors, at least.

I filled windowsills with houseplants, including epicia, cacti, African violets, and a lovely purple-blooming gloxinia from my coworker's collection. These plants were the closest thing to peace and order in that apartment building. As I had done years earlier in my disordered room back at my parents' home in East St. Louis, I had turned to plants for some balance to life among the scampering roaches, skirted men and an uncertain marriage.

After about a year at the paper, I discovered that I could double my salary by doing public relations for the school system. Despite the money, I lasted only about a year, arranging through then–managing editor Durwood McAlister to return to my old job. Back to the copy desk. Newspapering wasn't through with me yet.

Timing is everything. Soon after I returned, a *Journal* columnist was about to retire. The bosses decided to hold auditions for his spot on the editorial pages, inviting guest columns each week from anyone on staff and paying $25 per piece. I submitted one the first week about men who stood on Decatur Street downtown, waiting for work by the day, doled out by people driving by in trucks. Catching out, it's called. The column sold. As did a couple dozen after that.

Believing that I was on my way to the editorial board, I began dressing for success. Back to suits. After a month or so of this, no boss called to make me an offer off the copy desk. So I ditched the suits and resumed wearing full copy desk outfits. High caazh. Naturally, that meant I'd get a call directly.

Sure enough, one afternoon the copy desk phone rang, and publisher Jack Tarver was on the line.

"Lee, can you come up and see me?" he said.

I hoped that was the call I'd been waiting for, but had I known it was coming, I might've changed out of what I was wearing: red jeans, black shortsleeved jacket, no shirt. Sandals. Several rings, a bracelet and some sort of necklace with a marijuana leaf preserved in plastic. It was the '70s.

Whatever Mr. Tarver thought as I appeared before his massive wooden desk, he never blinked or did a double take, instead pushing on in his no-nonsense manner.

"You've been writing some good pieces," he began. "That one today about the music store closing was really touching."

I thanked him, and he went on. "I'm curious; are you writing these pieces for the $25, or are you interested in having your own column some day?"

"You know it's not for the $25," I answered, as we both chuckled.

"Well, you just keep writing."

How long? I wondered. I kept writing, getting comfortable with editorializing and wondering what it would be like to join an all-white editorial board.

Not long after my conversation with Jack Tarver, Hal Gulliver, editor of the *Constitution*, asked if I'd be interested in writing editorials and a column for that paper. Not the *Journal*, as I had expected all along. But I didn't hold out for my expectation, joining the *Constitution's* editorial board in 1975, writing twice, often thrice-weekly columns, in addition to writing unsigned editorials most days for the next five years. But before we shook hands on the deal, I had to have assurances that I would not be the race writer, confined to issues of special interest to black people at the expense of exploring broader topics.

Like most black people my age, I had seen a lot of black "firsts" and often was an "only," the only black student in English lit classes, the only black person in an expense-account restaurant. I was told that I'd be the first black member of the *Constitution's* editorial board. Like many black "firsts" I've known I felt good to break through a racial barrier but also some trepidation at being an "only."

Truth is, being an "only" can be more affecting than being a "first." Being this "only" on the South's premier newspaper would make me a lone target for years of hostility from those white readers who just couldn't stand to see one more wall torn down. Were any of us at the paper ready for this?

Fortunately, I didn't have to worry about hostility from inside the board among my colleagues, Gulliver, Bill Shipp, Gene Tharpe, John Raymond and cartoonist Clifford Baldowski. We easily divided up the opinion-writing, layout, page makeup and other duties in colorblind fashion.

Even though I did not want to be confined to race-writing,

race is too prominent in our society not to opine about it at all, and often when I did, lively debate arose, drawing in every type reader, from black ones bursting with racial pride to white ones laden with prejudice. Sometimes these arguments generated light, other times only heat.

Like any opinion writer, I was called a lot of bad names. And like any black opinion writer, mine sometimes were racial. I always knew to brace myself when I received a piece of mail with no return address and scrawling that was barely legible.

Never dull, often surprising, the job of telling people what to think was always stimulating and usually fun. By the time I left the job, I had grown skin three inches thick.

On the home front, my wife and I had our first daughter. After what seemed like days of labor, she finally arrived, soon after I had stared out the hospital window at a huge storm system rolling toward Atlanta from the west, spawning a tornado that did heavy damage. All of which inspired a nurse to dub her "Daddy's Little Twister."

Becoming a father again was much like being on a psychological bridge that spanned the space between my biological father and my first-born daughter. What did he think of becoming a father? Did he help my mother around the house while she was recuperating, as I did my wife? Would this new daughter ever get to know my first daughter? Would either know my father? This might be a good time to invite my first daughter, now eight years old, to visit us, I thought, but dismissed the idea, knowing how my wife disliked the idea of bringing that part of my past into our home. Eventually, I was to feel stronger and stronger about getting to know my first daughter. But not yet.

While Little Twister was still crawling, we bought our first home, a restored Victorian. This was a time when the American dream and expectation of owning a home could be met without strain. We saw, we bought, as not only a financial investment and physical shelter but as a symbol of our integration into the grownup community.

It was more house, more elegance than I'd ever had. I'd never even seen, let alone lived in, anything like it in East St. Louis: frame, painted in muted cream and gray, with gingerbread trim around the front porch. High-ceilinged, big-roomed with heart-pine floors.

As George Bush might have said: On track. Moving forward. To be sure, we were looking good. Two-income family, one child. We had a lot more going for us than Mother and Dad did. My hope was that, just as they found happiness with each other after having been married before, I would find joy in my second marriage, too. So much pleasure they would have gotten from our home, had they owned it. Years later, I wished I had been able to enjoy it the way it should have been enjoyed.

The place seemed a natural for gardening, and I set out to make it bloom. Indoors, I hung new ferns from the ceiling and continued growing other plants brought from the apartment. For the first time since I lived with my parents I gardened outdoors, planting corn, tomatoes, squash, okra and lots of herbs.

Indoors and out, nothing flourished. Nothing keeled over and died, but it didn't flourish. The vegetable garden yielded a few pieces of produce, while indoors the plants languished. The stately azaleas lining the home front hung in, as did a young plum at the corner of the front porch. Just staying alive.

For a while, I blamed low light for many of the plants' lack of enthusiasm. But years later, I grew plants in even less light. Eventually, I came to believe that the problem was something more complicated—some combination of my own lack of commitment to gardening at that home with that wife and the negative energy that plants picked up.

Like any other worthwhile endeavor, gardening is most

successful when it is fed with passion. But there was nothing in my marriage that inspired passion, at least good passion. My wife and I disagreed about things as small as whether the floors should be carpeted (I thought not but gave in when she argued that wood floors would be too cold for the baby) and as large as whether I should shun a married friend because of his relationship with another woman (no, I said).

Gardening always has been a peaceful pastime for me, and it always needed good passion, along with positive energy. Also, it has always given these attributes back to me when I've dug and planted and watered. Gardening is a whole, a symbiotic circle: to feel good, I have to garden. To garden, I have to feel like gardening. I don't have to feel rested, or even well, for gardening energizes. But I must feel willing. At that time, I simply did not feel like it. My life was not peaceful. Thus, I did not, could not, garden well.

Once again, gardening, or the lack of it, had become a metaphor for my personal life; marriage too, was languishing. The whispers I had heard in Cleveland were getting louder, as the bloom of passion faded.

Like the toothpaste that one partner fails to recap, small issues took on greater significance, indicating that something much more serious was wrong.

I disliked wall-to-wall carpeting covering the pine floors, but I did not care enough to argue about it. Similarly, I did not push for replacing drapes with a window covering that more easily admitted light, despite my desire for it. Arguing about such matters may be bad, but even arguing is better than not caring enough to argue. In much the same way, a relationship filled with bickering has more life than one characterized by total apathy. Eventually, I didn't care about the floors, and I didn't care about the windows.

As home wasn't fun, I spent long hours at work, stopped for drinks after work and wasn't much company when I came

home. For my own company, I made friends easily and eager-
ly, taking great pleasure in languid hours spent with women
who, I felt, understood me. We did not talk of future divorce,
focusing instead on present escapes. Such friendships gave me
a lift, affirming my continuing appeal, while not forcing me to
commit deeply. I liked knowing that I was desirable.

In fact, for many years, that was the silent question that I
always asked on meeting a woman: Don't you think I'm sensual? It is a question many men and women ask, in many ways.
It is how often we ask, how long, and what we do with the
answers that matters.

I knew there was a better life, having seen Mother and
Dad stay home with love. But I also knew I did not have that
life. And I saw no prospects for it. Going here and there did
not make up for that absence, but it sure diverted my mind
from it.

Beginning a pattern, I lived at the office, in a way. I virtually stopped gardening at home, but in my office in the editorial
department of the *Constitution*, I had some of the loveliest
plants anywhere. They hung from the ceiling, sat on my desk
and lined my window. I even had a croton bloom there.

I kept hearing the whispers, but like so many people, I
stayed married anyway, a long, long time past the time I
should have. Maybe it'll get better. It's better for our daughter.
Both were easy reasons. But inertia was a stronger bond than
either. And so I stayed.

And wrote, enjoying the freedom to range over every issue
imaginable in my op-ed page column. Politics, race, language,
food, education all were subjects that inspired.

Events in my life often were column material. An awful experience in late 1976 was such an example. East St. Louis was
barely clinging to life. Across the river, in Barnes Hospital, so
was Dad. Here's some of what I wrote about it:

Heart trouble, emphysema, pneumonia brought him to the

Mother and Dad, 1975. Connected by their souls.

eighth floor, to an area known as the "Coronary Care Unit."

To get in, visitors must lift a beige phone, identify themselves and enter one at a time. A sign on the door says, "In emergency situations visitors may be asked to leave."

Inside, he is lying there, this man who used to take me fishing, fix my bicycle and answer my child-questions. He is lying there with needles stuck in his swollen arms, an oxygen mask covering his mouth and nose. Wires are taped to his chest. His voice is only a whisper ("The tubes we had in his throat temporarily damaged his vocal cords," explains a doctor) and he is moving restlessly as I walk in.

Hospital visits usually frustrate me. Mostly because I feel so helpless and partly because I feel a little like I am imposing on the patient.

But when I saw Dad, part of me was glad I made this visit. His face smiled and his hands reached out to me in a show of gratitude for a trip that seemed to me the very least I could have done.

Another part of me was brought down, shattered, actually,

at seeing what illness had done. The man who taught me to drive the '41 Chevy could now not drive himself.

Random thoughts like that swept through me as I tried to cheer him and he tried to show he was being cheered. We talked of future visits and past events and present hope and the new year that was only a few days away.

My fifteen-minutes visiting time had ended and I was waiting for Mother to come out. She emerged tired, sighing, eyes glazed, barely fighting back tears. My old running buddy, Edward Buchanan, and I watched helplessly as she lost the fight and sobbed, "They think he may have had a heart attack. I just don't know if I can make it."

That seems to be the nature of sickness and of death. It is the survivors who always wonder if they can make it. Perhaps seeing loved ones struggling for life reminds us of our own vulnerability.

Back across the river in my erstwhile town, I am amazed at the proliferation of expressways, even while the town dies.

Night crashes, locking away this town like a giant jail door. And somehow fittingly my first night here is one of seven degrees with a north wind and three inches of snow.

It covers the town, obscures the ugliness and almost makes me believe the man across the river will get better.

Five months later, on May 12, 1977, at the age of fifty-eight, he was gone. Nine forty-two a.m., according to the death certificate.

I am convinced that from that moment on, Mother, whose very soul was connected to Dad's, began going down fast.

For my part, I thought harder than I had for a long time about my biological father and, for the first time, seriously, about my own mortality. In my thirties, I could still think of my gray hair as premature. But so was Dad's death. I wondered about my other father, the one living in Meridian—how he was doing, what was he looking like these days. When I looked in the mirror, I began wondering if I was seeing him in me.

During these years, travel was my friend, my coping mechanism. And so was running, which I took up in the mid-'70s, training many early mornings and entering ten-kilometer races on weekends. Both were handy escapes from home.

What a difference a couple of decades made. As a child soldier, I had trooped off to Europe with fun-filled expectations. I was traveling to something. Now, I was on the road to get away from something.

No story was too far or too tough. In 1978 I went on my first foreign assignment in newspapering, traveling for two weeks in Israel as a way of getting to know the country and the political and social issues surrounding it. The Golan Heights and the West Bank were impressive illustrators of the current regional tensions, but feeling the eerie majesty of the ancient battleground of Masada alone would have made that trip worthwhile.

And the miracle that the Israelis performed in making the desert bloom with oranges and vegetables was a wonderful sight. But a sad one too, as the lushness of these spaces, along with the calm, ancient stateliness of gnarled olive trees, stood in poignant contrast to the agitated state of alert that people lived in. Armed soldiers patrolled city streets. Civilians stashed Uzis under blankets on the back seats of their Mercedes. This was an exaggerated version of what life was like in America, with black people and white people armed against one another—sometimes with actual guns, sometimes only psychologically.

Just like in Birmingham, Alabama, or Meridian during the 1960s, at any moment, you could get bombed to death in the middle of downtown Tel Aviv. One day I was walking down a street there, when I heard a sharp explosion. Hitting the dirt, I lay there until I saw people gathering and smiling. The noise had been dynamite at a nearby construction site.

Such tension aside, the land, its people, its plants all reminded how much better education would be if only history and geography could be taught in the field instead of in classrooms.

The next year I saw the other side, visiting Jordan, Syria, Lebanon and Egypt while covering Jesse Jackson's efforts to bring peace to the region. I could not have guessed that, five years later, I'd be covering his run for the presidency. This was my first ride on what could be called Travels With Jesse.

My inauspicious beginning on that 1979 Middle East trip demonstrated the small hazards of the Arab-Israeli conflict. A hotshot international traveling journalist, I acquired two passports, one for Israel only and one for the rest of the world, as I had learned that some Arab countries frowned on issuing visas to passports that had been stamped in Israel.

When Jackson, his entourage and the group of journalists arrived in Beirut, our first stop, the Palestine Liberation Organization, then in charge, collected all passports. We checked into our rooms at the Wiener Haus hotel in an area alive with the sound of gunfire as factional fighting raged. In the hotel bar we journalists stood around soaking up booze and atmosphere, when, one by one, everybody but me had passports returned.

"Mustafa," I said to the PLO public relations man, "where's my passport?"

"Was something wrong with your passport?" he asked.

"Of course not," I said. Several reporters based in the region suggested ominously that maybe the PLO was planning to use my passport to cross into Israel and commit terror. Scenarios greatly enhanced by additional drinks had me envisioning a long, long stay in Beirut trying to sort out my legal problems.

A few minutes later, Mustafa and I repeated our earlier exchange, with his asking, "Are you sure nothing is wrong with your passport?"

The light bulb went on, and I dashed upstairs to my room,

attacked my luggage, and sure enough, I had given the PLO the wrong passport, the one for Israel only.

Sheepishly, I reported my discovery to Mustafa, giving him the other document. "No problem," he said.

Of course, there was a problem. Some days later, we were to get what Jackson had come for: a meeting with PLO Chairman Yasser Arafat, at one of the several homes he lived in, rotating residences to avoid harm or capture. Incongruously, as we walked across a plaza, we heard, wafting from a nearby upstairs window, strains of a disco hit, "You can ring my bellll-ll, ring my bell."

Arriving at Arafat's home, an elegant place with lovely paintings and a sumptuous feast, we took our places, Jackson sitting next to the chairman.

When I asked my first question, about whether the PLO could guarantee that its members would stop stashing bombs in Tel Aviv trash cans if Israel recognized Palestinians' right to a homeland, my passport blunder came back to haunt me.

"That is an Israeli question," declared an Arafat aide, glaring. Was he smiling too? I wasn't sure. I never gave anybody the wrong passport again.

At one point that night, Jackson, pointing at Arafat's pistol on his hip, said, "Mr. Chairman, I see you're packing your heat." Arafat looked puzzled, and Jackson continued: "Heat. In Chicago, we call that heat."

"Ohhhh," said Arafat, patting his weapon and flashing a big smile between his three-day growth, "Over here, we say this keeps the heat off."

In another linguistic moment, one that could have been embarrassing, Jackson gave an impromptu quote during a pickup basketball game in a Palestinian refugee camp in Amman. Urging both the Israelis and the Palestinians to communicate, he said, "We need a let's talk policy," but one white reporter heard "less talk policy." Sometime later, a few of us translated for him, but I never knew which version made it into his newspaper. I thought of ol' Ricky and the "dukes" back at IBM in Cleveland.

The trip had a lasting impact on me in at least one surprising way: it made me unlikely to insult other drivers on the road, as even back in the 1970s I saw traffic hassles in Beirut turn into shootings. Unfortunately, it was not long before America imported the custom. Riding around in PLO convoys at sixty miles per hour, with drivers waving their arms, blowing horns, flashing lights and shouting "Take it easy" to every other driver chilled me out. Since then, I have found few occasions urgent enough to drive as if my car were an ambulance.

Ask anybody why people drove like that, or why peace between Arabs and Jews was so elusive, and you get the same answer, one used to explain a world of strangenesses: "It's the Middle East."

It was in the Middle East that I saw an inspiring demonstration of why it always makes sense to order what you want in a restaurant instead of what you think is correct—as in cases when underlings wait to see what the boss is having. In Cairo, where Jackson had gone to meet with Anwar Sadat, a few of us reporters had a few minutes to spare, so we ate a few pieces of goat cooked on a grill set up in the street, then retired to an outdoor bar.

Somebody whispered something about not ordering alcohol because it would offend the Arab journalist among us. Religious grounds, as I recall. So, one by one, the reporters ordered Coke, orange juice, coffee. When my turn came, I ordered a gin and tonic, with lime. My colleagues' eyebrows raised critically. Then, the Arab ordered scotch on the rocks. He and I drank in the pleasure of watching the others' thirsty, longing eyes.

For me, one of the more magic moments of this trip was meeting Sadat, elegant in both personal style and professional demeanor. While Jackson and his people met with Sadat and his, we boys and girls (reporters) were served tea. At one point, we each got to say a few words to Sadat, who wore a black suit of lightweight cotton and straw sandals.

At the meeting's end, Jackson mentioned that he and his entourage might not be able to return to Beirut together, as they had scrambled for plane seats to make this hastily arranged meeting.

Sadat looked sympathetic, then snapped his finger to an aide, who trotted over. "My good friend the Reverend Jackson needs a plane," he said. "Get him my little ummmm, get him my little 737."

Flying out of Cairo in the president's plane was more of a kick than any of us had anticipated. There was almost one flight attendant for each passenger, and the food and drink were predictably fine. We were having a high old time until we entered Beirut air space and it hit us: we were flying in a plane that had "Egypt One" or something like that written all over it. This, of course, amounted to an enemy aircraft, flying into an airport controlled by freelance mortar shooters who might decide to take out a plane belonging to Sadat the "Israeli sympathizer." Happily, the landing was uneventful, but we sure lost our champagne highs.

Several of us got them back at a lovely restaurant, maybe the only lovely restaurant in Beirut in those days of mass destruction. French name. Le Grenier, I believe. For three hours, about a half dozen reporters sat at a table on the patio and grazed from a million little dishes of sauces, vegetables and meats, drinking bottles of dark beer and once in a while a gin and tonic with limes picked from the tree over our table.

I always think of that afternoon and that tree when I think of Beirut. The civility and beauty of the scene must have been the real Beirut. The killing and destruction were something else, something, I hoped, temporary.

Jackson's trip did not bring peace to the Middle East, of course, but it certainly gave me a good look at the region, its problems and people. No journalism school could have provided that. In journalism as in so much of life, there's nothing like the real thing.

The year 1979 also was the year I became a turpentine man. As part of a series called "The Underpaid and the Underprotected," examining several occupations, their low pay and lack of benefits, I went "undercover" in South Georgia, getting a job, using my full name, Eddie Lee May, joining an all-black crew working for a white business owner at the swamp-wading, back-aching, soul-breaking task of scraping gashes into pine trees, then collecting the gum that runs into metal cups attached to them, dumping the cups into buckets and dumping the buckets into fifty-five-gallon drums on wagons hauled by mules. In this ancient process, the gum is hauled to a distillery, where it is made into turpentine.

Working some sixty hours during the week among the water moccasins, mosquitos and horseflies, I was paid $42. This was a long way from the Ivory Tower of the editorial board, but it was a great story, a way to spend time away from home. The series won the 1980 Grand Prize in the Robert F. Kennedy journalism awards.

None of the agony of the work or the pleasure of the honor would have been possible had I been white. No one I talked to had ever known a white turpentiner, except those who owned the trees, distilleries and the profits. I was able to get the job in the first place because I altered my speech and body language (slurring and mispronouncing words, looking down) enough to convince the black recruiter I met at a service station that I was uneducated and desperate enough to take even the worse kind of work.

Having seen Mother come home after a long day of sweating and ironing at her laundry job, having seen Dad after his brutal days of breathing heat and paint fumes in his factory jobs, I knew something about the pain of doing the dregs of society's work. Unlike them, however, I could give mine up when I'd had enough.

Sometimes we journalists help people in those dreg-jobs, even when they do not want to be helped. My turpentine experience was, in some ways, one of those times.

By calling attention to what we considered deplorable conditions in turpentining and other jobs, including chicken processing and motel cleaning, we hoped to improve workers' lives. Ironically, some of the turpentiners, at least, expressed satisfaction at working in these grueling jobs, proudly noting that their fathers and their fathers' fathers also had been turpentine men, citing the solitary beauty of working alone in the woods and recalling how they'd tried other jobs but always returned to turpentining. The attention we focused on their industry, then, disrupted their work lives without truly liberating them. Were they "happy slaves"? I thought so. But without offering them better alternatives to what they had, I had no way of convincing them they were wrong.

By the end of 1979, my wife and I were parents again. I watched my third daughter's birth and wished that she was coming into a wonderful world, at least a happy home.

Happy or not, our home was headed for a shake-up. Jack Nelson, Washington bureau chief for the *Los Angeles Times*, had noticed my work for the *Constitution*, where he had once worked, and wanted me to join him in the nation's capital.

Jack's persuasive offer, combined with the fact that I had written every opinion I wanted to at least twice, made me decide to leave one of journalism's more desirable jobs: saying what you think and getting paid for it.

We moved to Washington in 1980, in the spring, when the city shucks off its serious gray facade and bursts into blooming color, showing off forsythia, cherry blossoms, azaleas, rhododendron and many pockets of special garden blossoms scattered through the town.

Actually, we moved to Virginia, to the suburbs. I've always

wondered why people hate to live in big cities but love to say they're from there. We wanted to live in the District but became Virginians because, like so many parents across America, we believed the 'burbs had better schools, more affordable housing and safer streets.

This move truly was fragmenting. I lived in Virginia, my office was in D.C., and I was employed by a California newspaper. But in a way that was fitting. My life was fragmented, too.

SUITCASE GARDENING

We moved into a house in a working-class neighborhood, a decidedly unfancy house, reminding me of how so many of us take steps backward in some ways in order to step up to the mountaintop of Washington. Lawyers, journalists, politicians, psychiatrists all aspire to practice in the nation's capital. For these and many other professions, making it in Washington is the test for the brightest.

Nevertheless, the question did arise: squeezing into a cramped old rental house in Northern Virginia—is this what I left a restored Victorian home and a comfortable job in Atlanta for? To live and work in places where virtually nobody knows my name? I brushed aside such questions, knowing that no matter how or where I lived, I worked in a town that some journalists thought was worth a lot more sacrifice than I had made.

Corresponding from Washington for a national newspaper was the perfect way to lead a fragmented life. I could work long hours, hang in the bars, travel broadly and run the area's streets and jogging trails in search of fitness and peace, a search that amounts to a kind of religion on the Potomac. Spending time at home did not figure highly in this equation, and I didn't know at the time what dissonance this omission created in my life. I didn't know how much I needed and wanted a home to love, a place I wanted to be and missed when I wasn't there. Not having, but needing, that played a sour note on my psyche. It was jangling.

While I often did not see them at night, I did usually visit with my daughters in the morning, helping them dress, preparing their breakfast and driving them to school.

Increasingly, I was living, emotionally, at the office, stashing my best-loved books in my desk, keeping a pair or two of shoes there as well. Friends knew to telephone me there instead of at home.

I hoped that buying a house would inspire some connection to home. I had brought a few plants from my Atlanta office and bought a few more in D.C. They all were at the house, as I only had a "pod" space at the office. I envisioned creating a garden at this suburban tract house, filling the lot with shrubs and trees, even training the dog to leave them in the ground.

Predictably, none of that worked out. The Virginia clay was too hard, and my will and desire too soft. I dug a few holes and put in a few random azaleas and rose bushes, then quit.

Instead of a garden, I had a little bad grass, along with a lot of great weeds. I cut, or had cut, whatever came up. And I didn't do that very often, feeling grateful for my late hours, as they prevented me from having to see hostile stares from neighbors who manicured their lawns.

On weekends, while my wife and children went to the skating rink, the swimming pool, the church, I spent my time running on a bicycle path and lounging on the sofa, watching football games. It is difficult for me to believe that I ever watched three football games in one day, as years later I found it difficult to watch even a quarter, aside from the Super Bowl. Clearly, in those days, the games, like so many of my activities, simply were good escape routes away from gnawing unhappiness.

We did try family outings from time to time: picnics, movies, dinners. I remember the meals with sadness. They were so telling. My wife and I would stare into the middle

The picture Mother didn't want.

distance, waiting for the waiter to break the silence with the presentation of food or the check. We were together but far apart. To our children, there'd be a, "Sit down" or, "Stop playing with your food." To each other, virtually nothing. What must our daughters have thought? I hope they knew this was not normal. Ever since those days, whenever I see a couple eating in silence, staring at nothing, I feel a tinge of pain for them.

Running about forty miles most weeks, I had lost what was left of the heavy weight I had put on during my insurance sales career. While in Cleveland, I became a vegetarian for a year, dropping from two hundred pounds down to about 175,

Running away — at 20-mile point in marathon (early 1980s in Wash-ington, D.C.).

even though I had mostly given up smoking. And now, with all the running, I was down to about 165. Gaunt.

During a White House function, I was photographed with President Reagan. When White House officials sent several copies of the photograph, I decided I'd send one to Mother. Despite my skinny frame, which would make her believe that I was not eating well, I knew she always was happy to get a pic. Not this time.

One day she called the bureau while I was out, and as was her habit, left a message that, "Your mother from East St. Louis" called.

When I called her back, I told her about the picture. Me with the president of the United States.

"Uh huh," she said quietly. "That's nice, son."

"I'm going to send you one. Not a bad shot. We're both wearing brown suits."

"Well, that's all right, you don't have to send me one."

"What? You don't want one? That's the first time you didn't want to get a picture of me."

"Well, yeah," she said, laughing at how she was imitating longtime family friend Tootie Fruity, who used that expression to start so many sentences. "You just keep that one. It's all right."

She explained that her dislike of Reagan's policies, such as appointments of conservative federal judges and the efforts to dismantle affirmative action programs, ran so deep that she could not in good conscience keep a picture of him in her home—even if I was in it too. She never saw the picture. However, she did force me to explain over and over why I was so thin. But never did she understand why any sane person would deliberately run for miles at a time.

"It allows me to eat and drink as much as I want," I told her, which was true.

All that running did get me into good enough shape to enter my first and only marathon, the Marine Corps, which I finished in three hours and forty-three minutes, urged on by *Times* colleagues and marathoners Ron Ostrow and Dick Cooper. The next day, I got up early and ran six miles, but my heart wasn't in it. I was growing tired of running as a means of getting away.

Going out of town on assignment was the ultimate escapism, literally.

I never said no to a story that meant travel. Mass murders in Pennsylvania on Saturday morning? Sure, no problem. Glad to do it. A couple of months in Atlanta to cover a murder trial? Sounds like fun to me. Three weeks on the campaign plane? You got it. Miami in the summer and Boston in the winter? Go ahead, make my rez.

I wasn't in Washington long enough to find a good sushi bar before I was off to Miami to cover riots and refugees, both of which that city had in abundance during the early 1980s.

My arrivals in this city always were a bit disconcerting. Invariably I'd be soothed by the resort-islandlike flora that grew so easily, so ubiquitously, but I'd be disturbed at the seething tensions that boiled over into violence again and again. The feeling recalled my trip to Beirut where the wonderfully convenient lime tree at the restaurant contrasted so vividly with the slaughter taking place so near. Beauty and beastliness.

From their own lush but ugly paradises Cubans and Haitians poured ashore in the spring of 1980, helping to doom Jimmy Carter's chance for reelection—once loved as an outsider, the incumbent president could do no right—as criticism mounted over how to stop the influx of immigrants and how to deal with them once they reached America.

Later that year, black Americans in Miami were outraged after an all-white jury acquitted four white policemen in the slaying of Arthur McDuffie, a black insurance man. Burning and looting and killing followed, and so did I.

One night, I visited a group of black residents of an apartment complex to get their views of the city's racial troubles. We sat in a small, dimly lit living room where a coffee table was filled with bottles of liquor. Tempers rose as the levels in the bottles fell.

"This is just a racist city," said one man. "Police ain't had no business killing that man in the first place. Now they gon' find 'em innocent."

This kind of talk went on for a while, and then flashing lights outside sent all of us scrambling to the front door. Pulled up in the yard, close to the apartment, was a police cruiser. Its doors and trunk lid all swung open and a half dozen officers flung themselves out, weapons drawn and pointed our way.

"What y'all doing here!" a woman shouted. "Who called y'all? Ain't nothin' goin' on here."

"Yeah, why don't y'all get the hell outta here. Go somewhere else," said another.

The cops looked itchy. "Take it easy," said one. "Everybody back inside," said another. Nobody moved. A long ten seconds passed. Then one of the policemen threw a tear gas canister. The unbearable stinging sent us all back inside, but the shouting continued, as the residents were then angrier than ever. Same for the police.

Maybe five minutes went by, while I pondered my next move. Stay there and risk getting rounded up and maybe worse after the angry cops storm the apartment? Shout, "Press!" and ease out of the neighborhood before anything happens? Fortunately, the cops cooled down before they could do anything more rash. They piled back into their cruiser and roared off, lights flashing, weapons ready.

It was my only gassing, other than those I got during Army training, when I could fumble into my gas mask. Getting gassed in anger is much worse. It made me think of how assiduously I had always avoided running afoul of the law. I hated the idea of being gassed or handled or hunted or handcuffed. And I especially hated the idea of being locked up in a cell, unable to see the sky or smell the flowers or to garden on my own terms.

Miami's suffering race riots long after those in other cities was just one example of how the South Florida town seemed stuck in the past. During those times, many black residents talked sadly and angrily of being politically powerless, even as other cities were electing black officials across the board in record numbers.

Yet, in some ways it was Every Town, U.S.A. While its furious building boom put up gleaming banks and hotels and office towers downtown, many of the poor black neighborhoods were the proverbial Tobacco Road, downtrodden, populated with shells of people, who shambled here and there, dead-eyed, hopeless, aimless.

For many of them, the neighborhood juke joint was the only respite from despair.

Miami seemed to have more juke joints than most cities, even more than East St. Louis, perhaps another indication of its stuck-in-the-pastness. One juke in a section of Miami called Overtown sticks in my mind. Dark, with a few tables, a bar lined with half-pint bottles and paper cups, and a high-volume jukebox jumping with old R & B hits, it smelled like Bourbon Street in the morning. The air conditioner was always turned up high enough to cool Miami's muggy air half a block down the street.

The place took me way, way back. Back to the dim, dank jukes I'd first known through Muddear and Dad in Alabama and Mississippi, then to those I'd found on my own in Georgia. This one was different because it had air conditioning. In most jukes, sweating was as much a part of the scene as the big jar of pig's feet sitting on the counter.

While the Miami joints took me back, that's not to say that everybody at these joints was stuck in the past. One man in a Liberty City juke walked up to me one night and offered to give me great quote about what he had seen during a riot if I would buy him a drink.

I said sure, and he said, "I drink Jack Daniel's. I know you can afford it 'cause you on expense account." He was right, of course. What he came up with was a quote morsel, not the five-course feast he had promised. But at least the Jack Black was good.

During these long, frequent trips, I was gardening out of a garment bag, just as I was living out of one.

To satisfy some vestigial gardening urge, I carried in my bag a little white ceramic vase, shaped like a six-inch-high paper sack, complete with little ridges on top. In each hotel, as soon as I got to my room, I would take out the little bag-vase and set it down on a table, next to the bottle of Remy Martin VSOP. Then I would strike out in search of pothos or philodendron. In most large hotels these were as commonplace as the deodorized smell that always jumped into my clothes. One of these vines usually trailed over the balcony on every floor. Sometimes I'd have to go to the lobby and pinch from pots.

Back in my room with my booty, I'd put it in the little vase of water and sit back with a little snifter of yac, eyeing my prize and imagining that I had just planted an extravagant garden. That was as close to having one as I would come in the early 1980s.

During one particularly long road trip—about ten weeks in Atlanta in late 1981 and early 1982—I was covering the trial of Wayne Williams, convicted of killing two young men among more than two dozen victims linked in the infamous "missing and murdered" cases. While the chilling courtroom testimony and the scramble to report and write were stressful, they had not prepared me to cope with the loss of my bag-vase.

One evening, after court had adjourned, I dashed into my room to write and file, and noticed immediately that the vase was gone. Just as the pothos had begun to root during my marathon stay. Looking around, I found neither plant nor vase. Fortunately, the *Times'* West Coast deadlines gave me time to search. After several calls to housekeeping, I persuaded someone to comb through the trash bins. An hour later came the welcome knock on my door.

"Mr. May, we found your, er, vase," said the delivery man, trying to keep a straight mouth.

"Thank you very much," I said, pressing a five-dollar bill into his hand, which wiped the smirk right off his face.

At times the trips helped me see family members, as I had assignments in or near East St. Louis from time to time. And on one trip to Chicago, I had dinner with my eldest daughter and my first wife. Happily, it was pleasant, without even an undercurrent of rancor. This dinner was a giant step toward a relationship between my daughter and me, one that was long overdue. She was about sixteen at the time. I did not want to wait until she was in her forties.

If that meal was a giant step forward for my daughter and me, her visit to my home one summer was a step backward for my second wife and me. During the entire week, my wife barely talked with my daughter, hardly even addressed her, hurting and embarrassing me. My two younger daughters, meanwhile, got along splendidly with their new-found sister, but they did not see one another often over the years.

My willing mobility reached its zenith in December 1983, when Jesse Jackson was preparing to go to Damascus to negotiate the release of captured Navy flier Lt. Robert Goodman, whose plane had been shot down over Syrian-held territory in Lebanon.

Times Washington Bureau Chief Jack Nelson called me into his office on the day Jackson was scheduled to leave and said, "Lee, I want you on that trip."

"I'll try, Jack," I said, noting that our bosses in Los Angeles had decided to pass. "I don't have a visa, and they're leaving in a few hours."

"I know," said Jack. Then he added, in a way that let you know he felt he could be on that plane, even if he had only five minutes to get his visa from the recalcitrant Syrians, "But the *L.A. Times* needs to be there. That's gonna be a helluva story."

"Damn right," I said. "And a helluva trip." I summoned a taxi to take me to my Virginia home, had the driver wait while I dug out my passport and threw a few clothes in a bag, dashed to the Syrian Embassy, got the visa and hooked up with Jackson's people with time to spare.

Once again, I was covering Jesse Jackson in the Middle

East. More Travels With Jesse. But this time, it really was the beginning of his presidential campaign. Springing Goodman certainly couldn't hurt.

As always, following Jackson was an adventure, including the threats to *New York Times*man Ron Smothers and me as we strolled around a building brandishing tape recorders while Syrian soldiers, known as Pink Panthers because of the pinkish spots in their camouflage uniforms, brandished automatic weapons. We had a communications problem, but the rifles and pistols helped Ron and me understand pretty quickly. We put away the recorders.

During the many talks between Jackson and various factions, a few reporters retired to the hotel restaurant one evening, when I had my first and only raw calf brains, which were presented with a wonderful flourish. Alas, before I could finish, we were summoned by Jackson to his room, where he, shoeless, briefed us on his latest chats—as he ate.

When Jackson accomplished his mission, forcing President Reagan to acknowledge that a freelancer had scored big diplomatically, the scramble was on among the boys and girls to write the big story. Roaring out of Damascus on a windowless cargo plane, we scribbled furiously for hours on yellow pads. For most of us this was still BC (before computers).

Stopping at the U.S. airbase in Frankfurt to change planes and file stories, Ron and I, along with a *Washington Post* reporter, dashed to phones in the officers' club, got our respective recording machines on the lines and dictated:

". . . Goodman . . . rescued . . . flew home to freedom. Period, paragraph. New graph, open quote . . . close quote. . . ."

Later, I wished I had a tape of our triple staccato dictation because it came to feel so old and real, compared to the ever-changing, technology-saddled journalism that we all take for granted now. Drained, we made our way to the next plane, one with windows, and hunkered down, preparing for the flight home. It was cognac time.

* * *

In 1984, I was part of a tag-team assigned to cover Democratic presidential candidates, an assignment best described as daily foraging for a good quote and a good meal. Actually, a few other objectives could be listed as well, including a good drink and stimulating company. Sometimes company came in the oddest ways.

One night in a bar in Manchester, New Hampshire, I was looking only for a good drink. I found it and settled back to watch the people. Even better than watching people is watching people watch people. I did that too. Little did I know that three people seated to my right were watching me. A man and two women, all in their forties.

As this was the presidential season in New Hampshire, I never expected to see "civilians" in this hotel bar, only journalists and political operatives. But these clearly were civilians. The man started a conversation, and the women joined in. We talked a lot of politics, of course, but also music, literature and, near and dear to my heart, food and gardening.

Turned out he was married to one of the women, and the other was a family friend. To my amazement, he quietly suggested that I accompany them home—they lived in the area—for more drinks.

Worn out from a long day and just slightly wary, I didn't go. But the group seemed nice enough, so I did take down their telephone numbers. And later, I telephoned the single woman. She turned out to be a very good friend, teaching me much about the region and being a confidente when I needed one.

She and other women helped me understand why I have always loved the company and friendship of females: they help me explore a range of relationships that could never be possible for me with a man. From casual friendship to love to sex without love—all these and more relationships are possible, including those that focus solely on professional matters or on sports or war. A good woman is easy to find in all those areas.

At one particularly stressful time, when I was trying to figure out how long I could keep running away from home, I telephoned her from Baltimore, caught the next plane to Boston and drove to New Hampshire. We went for a picnic on a hillside and talked and gazed out on the trees and shrubs and a little church steeple rising above a few dozen homes. For that moment, at least, life was at peace. I did not dwell on the fact that I had had to run away again to get there.

The grind of campaign coverage gave everybody out there handy excuses for wallowing in decadence, although decadence seems to have fallen on hard times among latter-day reporters who drink more Evian than Jack Daniel's and think cold cereal beats a full-cholesterol breakfast.

At the *Los Angeles Times*, where there were still a few ol' decadent scribes around, we would follow a would-be president for a few weeks, then hand off to a colleague. Mondale, Hartpence, Jackson, Hollings, McGovern, Cranston, Askew all were our targets. And, of course, John Glenn, space hero. One Democratic party loyalist looked at the field of candidates and dubbed it "Jesse and the Sominex Seven."

No wonder. Jackson's campaign easily distinguished itself from the others in the fervor it engendered in his supporters, who would wait for hours in tiny churches, then stand on the pews and holler and stomp when he arrived, late as he wanted to be. Never mind that he had never run anything in government, his supporters said, the man can deliver a speech. Even if he didn't have a clue about how to deliver good government.

And who else would have the audacity to take a campaign to Panama, Nicaragua and El Salvador to discuss regional issues, then dash off to Cuba, meet with Fidel Castro and come away with a planeload of political prisoners.

During that jaunt to Havana, I could not resist this exchange with Castro as he strolled through our plane, shaking hands with reporters:

"Buenas dias, Señor Castro. Me llamo Lee May. Soy de Cuba."

"De Cuba?" said a surprised Castro.

"Si, Cuba . . . Cuba, A-la-BA-ma."

He rocked back in laughter and rolled on through the plane.

I did not cover Jackson during the time it was being reported that he referred to Jews and New York City as "Hymie" and "Hymietown," but I saw him one night when he and my candidate were at the same event, and he appeared drawn and tense. By the time my turn to follow him came around again, he seemed in fine form. And even after the reports, his supporters remained fervently loyal. Once, at a campaign rally in North Carolina, I heard a woman say frantically, "Where is he? Where is he? I just want to touch the hem of his garment."

The space man was my man in February. As one of a merry band of bus-bound journalists, I traversed the towns and hills of New Hampshire, chronicling Glenn's comings and goings, his tilting at success and at humor.

Contributing to Glenn's political failings and to my personal happiness was his habit of starting his day at a civilized hour. On this day in February, that meant that at 7:25 a.m., in Nashua, Glenn and us boys and girls were still in the hotel.

Watching nearby Boston's WBZ-TV, I saw Linda Harris anchoring the station's local news, the "cut-in" of the "*Today* Show."

Impressive. I liked that she did not smile inappropriately, as some anchors do when reading something like, "Seven dead, a gunman in custody." At the same time, she did not perform the stories or deliver bad news with its gravity on her face and in her voice.

I liked her work and telephoned the station to tell her so as soon as the five-minute newscast was over. When she returned my call ten minutes later, I was still in my room, not having to be at a Glenn event for another hour. And it was a yawner in the hotel.

So we talked, mostly about news and politics. After that, I'd telephone Linda from various campaign stops—places like Birmingham, Chicago, New York. We'd still talk about journalism and politics, the absurdities in each, but we also branched out to topics like '55 Chevys and old rock 'n' roll. We both were happy and relieved that the other was old enough to remember "golden oldies" from Chuck Berry and Sam Cooke and Dinah Washington and Little Richard, and to know that Wings was not Paul McCartney's first singing group.

"Who's the hardest working man in show business?'" I asked her at one point during our feeling-out days.

"That's too easy," she said, "The Godfather of Soul."

"Good God!"

If I called while she was writing for her noon newscast, she might say, "Listen to this lead and tell me what you think" or "I can't believe that Mondale really believes he's going to be president after that speech he made last night."

This went on for a year. We did not meet during that time, maintaining a telephone friendship and a nonchalance about what kind of relationship we might build.

By 1985, I, like all the Democratic presidential candidates, was off the campaign bus. Reagan was back for four more years, and I went on to other stories, including one about the working poor and how the harder they worked the behinder they got because of tax laws that made them pay on their meager earnings and welfare laws that kicked them off assistance as soon as they made a little money. To illustrate the story, I, with help from a social worker, found a poor but determined working family in North Carolina.

The piece drew numerous letters and telephone calls, including a call from television producer Steven Bochco. He was moved by their plight and wanted to help the family by sending a check. As he did not want them to know who their benefactor was, Steven asked me to run his check through my account and send the family one of mine. Sure, I said, I'll launder the money. The $5,000 check absolutely overwhelmed the family with gratitude; it was about a year's worth of earnings—before taxes. He made a lifelong impression on them and a lifelong friend of me.

The beauty of thriving friendships is that they do not demand or promise anything extraordinary. Yet many deliver important life lessons. From the first, this was one of those, even though, living on opposite coasts, we never saw each other frequently.

Steven shows that a busy, high-stakes work schedule is no reason to bypass life's simple joys, such as walking a hillside and marveling at cactus blooms, interestingly shaped rocks or a speedy jack rabbit. I saw him connected to these natural beauties during a weekend in New Mexico, when I knew that he was in the middle of hashing out important issues surrounding a new television series.

Peerless as a powerful, creative talent in television drama— "Hill Street Blues," "L.A. Law," "NYPD Blue" are some of his works—Steven demonstrates as well as anyone I know the ability to enjoy a moment or day of pleasure without mentally checking out or checking the clock, even though he knows it is ticking on his many work projects. I asked him how he manages to do such a good job of separating work from play, compartmentalizing each.

"That's part of the process of growing older," he told me, "and not wanting to burn out. One thing I've learned: in my job your work is never done—no matter how long you stay at the desk, no matter how many days you work. Once you realize that, it's easy to walk away from it. And when you go some place to relax, decide you're going to be in that place. And be there. What's the point of working as hard as you work and not enjoying it?"

Works for me.

When I began work on a story about higher education, I asked myself, where better to report this story than in Boston, where there seems to be a college on every other corner?

Finally, in February 1985, a year after first meeting by telephone, Linda Harris and I would meet in person. But only for a drink, no meal. Neither of us was interested in starting something that was destined to go nowhere, since we were both married. Sure, the phone chats had been good for both of us, especially since we hadn't hit on each other. At least we didn't know we had. Anyway, we each believed that actually seeing one another would end the relationship anyway, as we couldn't possibly like one another nearly as much in person as we had on the telephone.

Wrong.

At Linda's suggestion, I had taken a room at the Parker House, down the street from her apartment, where she stayed during the week, spending weekends at her home in nearby Beverly.

It was Sunday night. My bag-vase was in place, interviews scheduled for the next day. The meeting with Linda was on.

At the appointed time, 8 p.m., I was standing in the hotel lobby, looking around, when I heard a warm, soft voice in my left ear: "Lee May?"

Uh oh, I thought as I turned to see this lovely woman who was as charming off camera as on.

"Yes," I said, realizing she hadn't a clue about what I looked like. Of course I had seen her from only the waist up. Now I saw much more. Her thin, five-foot-seven-inch frame was wearing, really wearing, a pair of leather pants and a short fur jacket, her hair was curly, her eyes expressive and her mouth full. I loved her lips. We made our way to the bar, which was dim and cozy.

Linda and Lee soon after meeting.

When the waiter came to take our orders, Linda surprised me by ordering one of my favorite winter drinks, Jack Daniel's on the rocks. Same for me, I told the waiter.

Disconcerting as it was to both of us, we were having as much fun in the flesh as we had had over the telephone lines.

We exchanged war stories from our journalism travels; I'd always loved knowing a woman who had her own. And we exchanged dreams of being in places at times that had nothing to do with journalism. Australia or New Zealand would be a nice place for an amateur archeology dig, Linda believed. Kyoto, watching the moss grow on the temple, for me.

We learned much that we had not discovered in our periodic chats. I discovered that much of the time that she had been talking to me, Linda probably was asleep, as I had no qualms about ringing her up from western time zones when it was midnight in New England. That might have been OK, but she awoke daily at 3:15 a.m. to make her first newscast at 5:30 a.m. She never told me what an inconsiderate fool I was for calling her so late. She just learned to sound awake even if she was not.

Also, we learned that, as much as we loved talking about those old R & B songs, the music of our youth, we also had in common a longtime love for European classical and for country—something we each had developed over the previous decade or so.

It was natural. If we loved the blues, and we did, we couldn't help loving country. Both kinds of music tell the same stories through the same kind of songs. They tell it happy, and they tell it sad—hard times, good times and bad times: hurting songs, cheating songs, drinking songs, traveling songs, loving songs, somebody-done-somebody-wrong songs. And in both kinds of music, we could understand the words.

We also could understand the values. Country and blues both are roots music, music that connects us to our people and to our places. Both deal with plain, simple times, basic endeavors, earthly pursuits. Like digging in the dirt.

So we talked about Waylon and Willie and Reba and Patsy and a whole slew of singers and pickers who turned us on, how new country was beginning to sound too much like rock or elevator music, how a lot of our black friends were closet country lovers and how at our ages there's no reason to be in the closet about anything in life.

Our just one drink turned into a meal and a long, exciting evening of conversation. We talked and ate and drank each evening until I had reported the education story and was gone back to Washington and to Virginia.

The trip told both of us what we couldn't have predicted, that we'd be happy if we lived together. It was an incredibly big if. At the same time, I had discovered an incredibly strong feeling. The first time we kissed, I felt what I had longed to feel all my adult life, but didn't believe existed: a desire and a need to love just one woman.

We were both married, lived and worked in separate cities and knew that changing any of those facts would be tough, let alone changing all of them.

For both of us, life may not have been happy, but it was safe and predictable. And for Linda, it was in many ways quite comfortable and well-connected.

Teaching at a local college, on the board of another, anchoring early morning and noon newscasts at the top station in a large, lively TV market after several years of traveling the world to produce and host a popular syndicated travel series, she was loved, respected and well paid.

Separated amicably from her husband, she divided her time between the downtown Boston apartment and the family home near the ocean in Beverly. As she had lived in New England for twenty-some years, she had numerous close friends with whom she had practically grown up. And she had raised two lovely daughters, Camian and Leslie, who were still in Massachusetts, along with Camian's husband, John. Life could have been a whole lot worse. A prospective grandmother, Linda did not relish leaving all this, and she certainly wasn't looking for a series of traumatic life-changes.

Neither was I. My life wasn't nearly as desirable, but it was safely fragmented, and I had settled into acceptance of that fragmentation, discovering the awesome power of apathy to numb the soul to pain.

We did it anyway, as we knew we would, as we knew we had to, launching into massive upheaval of our lives in order to live together. At forty-something (she was born eight months before me), we weren't about to let this chance go by, nor were we going to wait years while we thought about it. Of course, some very dear friends of Linda's thought that was exactly what she should do, believing she was rushing into trouble that would break her heart.

And among my friends, there were skeptics, too.

Two buddies, Michael Cottman in New York and Michael Yamamoto in Washington, had watched with interest and curiosity the progression of my romance with Linda. Eventually, Cottman had business in D.C., so the three of us got together for dinner at an Ethiopian restaurant.

About six glasses of tej and three beers into the meal, one of the Michaels said, "So, you're really serious about Linda, huh?"

"Yup."

"Does this mean you won't be hanging out and running the streets anymore?" said the other Michael.

"That's right," I said. "I'm hanging up my spikes."

There was a moment of silence, after which a Michael said, "We hereby dub you Caninus Emeritus."

Somberly, we three raised our glasses. I was honored. And pleased to be off the streets and out of running.

While I was glad to know so clearly that I was heading for happiness, I was sad about the prospect of another divorce, and I feared that leaving my wife would anger her so much that she would throw up roadblocks to my contact with our two daughters.

Soon after Linda and I met, I telephoned Mother to tell her the news. What she gave me was the kind of succinct assessment about important matters in life that only comes from the mouths of mothers.

"Mother, this is it," I said. "She's the one. I know it. We're going to get married, and it's going to last."

"I hope so, son, 'cause you can't keep doing this."

Mother's wisdom was just as sharp during a telephone conversation with Linda. Making the call, Linda was understandably nervous, not knowing if Mother would perceive her as a homebreaker, a bad woman. When Mother answered the telephone, Linda hesitantly announced herself and asked how Mother was doing.

There was a little pause, after which Mother chuckled and replied, "I'm doing fine, Sugar, how you?" Then she laughed a little more, and Linda joined in. Pretty soon, they both were roaring. Fun, relief, joy all were a part of their kindred laughter. During their conversation, Linda raised the question of "homebreaking," telling my mother that she didn't want to break up a happy family. Sadly, we were not happy, Mother reported.

Later, Linda talked about how much she appreciated Mother's understanding. "In that one moment," Linda said, "she showed me that she was not judgmental, that she understood and knew I was not a bad person. I appreciated her wisdom, her womanness."

Then, paying me a high compliment, Linda said, "You were so fortunate to be raised by a mother like her. I do think it helps explain why you are so comfortable with women."

Amid the skepticism, good wishes, bad predictions and motherly advice and understanding, we rushed into wholesale change with abandon, exchanging visits, telephoning and writing and planning.

On one beautiful summer day in the nation's capital, we hunted a home, looking at about a dozen, selecting one on Capitol Hill. In early November, while Linda was still in Boston closing down her affairs, I moved in, supervising the building of a wall of bookcases and cabinets by the most unusual craftsman I've ever known.

Maybe, considering that I had just left a wife and two children after fourteen years of marriage, a parting that was gut-wrenching sad and, in some ways, scary—change of any kind so often is—maybe I needed the tall, skinny, soft-spoken carpenter for diversion.

In any case, I got him. He started off fairly normal, measuring the wall space for the cabinets and shelves, then bringing in his tools and materials and getting down to business. After about a week, he declared that he was running behind schedule and had better move into the basement in order to work longer hours and save commuter time.

Fine with me. So he began working until two and three in the morning, tuning up his saws and hammering away, long after Johnny Carson had said goodnight. I wasn't about to complain; craftsmen were too hard to find in D.C.

Then, he escalated. One afternoon I came home from the office to find him taking a load of laundry out of the dryer. He was wearing a caftan and an I'm-beginning-to-feel-really-at-home look. I was OK with that; I thought it was a little strange, but I was OK.

He had crossed the line, however, when I came home to find him about to use one of the iron skillets I'd just bought. He was about to heat an order of shrimp-fried rice he'd bought down the street. I hadn't even used the skillet. I hadn't even had time to season it. That was it. He could sleep in the basement, work all night and wash caftans in the washing machine. But he couldn't mess with my iron skillets. Those were my blue suede shoes.

When I told Linda how I'd snatched the skillet off the fire just before the shrimp-fried rice hit it, she laughed nervously, fearing I was going to fire the guy just before he finished the project. "Don't do that," she said from Boston. "You know how hard it is to get anybody to do work."

I didn't. He pushed on, but was still working when Linda moved in a few weeks later. In fact, he was vacuuming the carpet even as the moving van with Linda's furniture pulled up in front of our rowhouse.

Our rowhouse. Our home. I loved the sound of it. And the feel of it was right, spiritually, even if it was carpeted and mostly beige. It felt right for us because it was a unifying force. It meant I could bring the little items home from the office, the books, the shoes. Finally, all my stuff could be in one place.

Before Linda moved to town, I had moved in Sarah Frond, our first plant, a Boston fern. Not all our plants received names, but she demanded one. Huge, majestic, she hung in the front window, waving at the passing buses. She was the only plant in the house, the only thing, other than the cabinetmaking tools and two bar stools.

When the moving van was unloaded, Sarah had company. Linda had brought several African violets that she was growing in Beverly. We put them on shelves in a little sunroom off the kitchen, adding a few other plants that we picked up in Washington. Thus, we were off and rolling toward a massive collection of indoor plants.

Outdoors, I happily dove into landscaping our postage-stamp-size front yard, building a little garden that contained a pine, a tree-form photinia, hydrangea, chrysanthemum, three azaleas, six ferns and a stone. With those, there was no more room.

Out back, the only earth was in a brick trough about eighteen inches wide and six feet long. I put a few perennials in it, including carnation, liatris, lavender and artemisia, along with a camellia and a gardenia. On the little brick patio, I grew a variety of potted plants, such as ferns, roses, forsythia, Japanese maple and Japanese black pine. They thrived.

Indoors, I got loose, trying to grow enough houseplants to make up for the shortage of space outdoors. Trying to make up for the years I had not really gardened.

We thought we had reached critical mass several times, but every time I thought there might be no room for a new baby, I'd find a way to accommodate it.

From Linda's sweet lips sarcasm dripped one day when she came home to find a huge snake plant blocking the doors to the washer and dryer closet.

"So, we have to move that plant each time we need to do a load of laundry?" she asked. "Or should we start sending it out?"

And she smiled when she pulled up in front of the house one evening to see me through the window, standing on a table watering a group of newcomers that had found homes hanging from the ceiling.

Talk about fun. I was having it. To be gardening again, really gardening, felt in some ways like my finally discovering higher education at Southern Illinois University. It was a feast for my soul, smorgasbord. I couldn't get enough. Finally, I had a space I could fill in completely. At last, I had reached a point in life, found a relationship, that made gardening feel right. I was home.

There were adjustments, as in any new living arrangement. For one thing, I was not prepared for Linda's high level of neatness. How high it was came through one night when she bounded from the bed, swept over to a closet and closed its door—a door I had left open.

"I lay there and tried to ignore it," she said. "But I couldn't.

It bothered me, and I figured you might as well know that about me now because you'd find it out later."

OK, I said, no problem, not suspecting that her penchant for order would affect me as much as it wound up doing. I actually grew to like it, a huge change for someone who once threw barbecue bones and beer cans on the floor near the bed.

My newfound love of order had effect at the office, too. Like most desks in newspaper offices, mine was piled high with five-year-old press releases, congressional studies that never saw the light of legislation, assorted notebooks, speeches, message slips and mail. One day, I looked at this mess and saw disorder, a condition that I decided was affecting my mind as well as my space.

So I began throwing away stuff, eliminating a few inches at a time from the bottom of the pile. After I threw away each batch, I'd wait awhile to see if I ever needed anything I'd discarded, or if anyone ever called and asked me about any of it. Neither ever was the case. Eventually I got rid of the whole pile, leaving an incredibly spare desk. Somehow the space clearing acted as a mind clearing as well. Work seemed more manageable.

I applied the same technique to my closets at home, giving to charity any item of clothing that I had not worn for two seasons.

Another of our adjustments had to do with territoriality. We discovered just how disconcerting it can be to get what you want.

By the time Linda and I met, we both had become accustomed to operating like lone managers around the house. In her previous life, she pretty much bought the furniture, food and furnishings without consultation, knowing her husband wouldn't opine against it. Similarly, in my previous life, I almost never weighed in on purchases for the home—unless they were plants, which I considered my personal passion.

Certainly, we both had wished for a relationship in which each partner cared equally about what went into the home and into the ground around it. That, we figured, would reflect a caring relationship.

We got our wish when we got together; we also got some surprises. The first one came during a shopping trip to the Virginia suburbs, where we went hunting a ceiling lamp. There must have been a million of them in the place, but eventually we narrowed down the possibilities to two.

"We'll take that one," Linda said, pointing to my second choice.

"Whoa," I said. "I like the other one. Let's flip for it."

She has always loved telling that story, saying she was taken aback that I had an opinion about the lamp, adding that she believed up to the end that I was kidding about letting a coin decide.

When the quarter came up heads and I asked the clerk for our lamp, we both knew that we had entered, for us, uncharted territory.

While Linda was surprised and undone that I cared enough to beat her out of her lamp choice, I also was surprised (and delighted) to learn that what went into the house mattered to me. A lamp is just an object, like a carpet or a set of drapes, yes, but this one represented a commitment to being involved in shaping our space, a desire to have some of me there.

Along with the happy learning experiences, there were, of course, prices to pay.

Linda was able to stay with her broadcasting company, Westinghouse, but she took a huge pay cut and had to host a talk show in Baltimore, the closest job available in the company. Thus, she commuted a hundred miles a day. She had left her many longtime friends to live in a city where she had few and saw little prospect for making more, as she felt Washington was a cold town to "outsiders."

To be sure, many people in Washington automatically sniff dog tags (the ubiquitous identification tags worn around the neck of government officials and journalists) before deciding whether someone is anyone. And Washington is the only city where you can hear this pickup line in a bar: "Hi, I'm a GS-15. What do you do?" What you do is far more important than who you are. People introduce themselves this way: "BobThompsonStateDepartment" or "BrendaMusgroveChicagoLightPress."

To the uninitiated, they might be Bob Department and Brenda Press.

While Linda was fighting to find her way around the Beltway, I was agonizing over the emotional cost of seeing my two daughters. After I left, I tried visiting them, but it went badly. I felt like a "McDonald's Daddy," one of those fathers whose only time with his children is at a fast-food restaurant. Or maybe the zoo.

Their mother had told me she didn't want them to visit the home where I lived with "that woman." Apparently she had told the girls, too, because once when I picked them up and stopped by the house to pick up something, they declined my offer to wait inside the house. After months of visits during which I would be warned—in front of our daughters—not to take them to my home (despite court orders to the contrary), I became nervous and angry before each visit. Eventually I stopped, concerned that to continue would damage our children and make it impossible to have a relationship with them anytime in the future. This experience proved that a court cannot always legislate family relationships.

Such stresses of upheaval in our lives did take a toll on our relationship at times. When Linda came home one night in tears after being lost somewhere between Baltimore and D.C., my heart ached for her. And when I went to visit my children one Saturday, then returned in an incredibly short time, visibly shaken at the awkwardness of being a visitor with my daughters and the contentiousness of my relationship with their mother, Linda hurt too. Such occasions made us tense, snappish and sad all at the same time, ruining evenings and making days seem longer. Times like these made me wonder if she was missing her old, safe life with the men friends of whom I had been briefly jealous. And Linda wondered if I was feeling that being separated from my children was too big a price to pay for this new relationship.

A metaphor for this kind of struggle was a shopping visit to a mall in suburban Maryland. Starting our new life together, we gaily bought lots of towels, sheets, pillows and other household items, which were loaded into several huge plastic bags. We lugged our purchases to the parking lot and started for our car. We couldn't find it. We searched for five minutes, then ten, twenty. After about half an hour, we were dazed, hurt, tired and disgusted. Was this to be the fate of our search for happiness in a new life?

No. Fortunately, we never wavered in our belief that we had done the right thing. We knew we wouldn't be lost always. But we have never liked malls since that night.

Experience in life and the certainty that we loved each other helped us get through such times without blaming each other. We knew the changes we made would not always happen smoothly. Similarly, I tried to avoid making my children pay for the problems of their parents. I wrestled with whether to continue visiting them, even if bad feelings flared between their mother and me. I decided against that, hoping that they eventually would feel comfortable and free to visit me. At that time, they, both under twelve years old, did not.

Regardless, I vowed that I'd never miss a support payment for them. I never missed one.

Meanwhile, my eldest daughter, by my first marriage, was cautious, suspicious at first, about my new relationship, but slowly she decided that Linda and I were good together and became part of our family.

Moreover, I gained Linda's daughters, Camian and Leslie. And her sister Carol and her daughters, Dana and Lauren. There was Camian's husband, John, Dana's Tom, Lauren's Steve. With age, family ties were growing—and growing more important.

As was gardening. In some areas, years really do instruct. Perhaps it is recognition of our own mortality that impels us to increase our connections to friends and loved ones as we age, an effort to make up for lost time and lost opportunities. Or maybe it is a drawing inward, a tightening of the circle of loved ones that pushes us. Whatever the impetus, the change comes with age for most. It did for me.

Just as I increasingly appreciated relationships as I headed toward fifty, I gained far more pleasure from gardening than I ever had. Of course, finding a happy relationship was crucial to my gardening with any passion at all. But aging was a supercharger, adding thrust to my passion. Fortunately, aging and enjoying a relationship arrived at around the same time. Things happen right sometimes. The convergence made me feel brand-new—both as a gardener and as a lover. I was in my forties, but I was younger than I had been ten years earlier.

Speaking chronologically, age brings a tendency to contemplate life's gifts, and gardening is the perfect way to do that. As young ones we are less inclined to savor, as most of us felt we had little to savor.

Patience is part of what makes gardening better with age, (though even we older gardeners lose it sometimes). Ironically, patience increases even as time shortens. Having seen so many starts without finishes, we like to wait and see a thing jell—a huge attribute in making a seed or seedling or cutting into a large plant.

Cuttings and seedlings both went into our little garden on Capitol Hill, a few blocks east of the Capitol. Remembering Mother's saying that plants should be gifts or simply "pinched," I started the forsythia from a little twig I broke off a showy hedge at Union Station. A corkscrew willow growing in a pot was only a wisp when I bought it. Patience saw them through.

Plant shopping trips sometimes were poignant. Linda and I went to Merrifield Garden Center in Virginia to buy our first Japanese maple. We had talked about how few black people we saw during our trips to nurseries, and how we saw even fewer black men. On this occasion we met a black man, who must have sensed our pleasure—in that way that black people often do when encountering one another in unexpected places.

We struck up a conversation that, on its face, was nothing special—interesting plant, nice shape; yes, great for small spaces because it grows slowly; wish they were less expensive—that kind of thing. But underneath that, the conversation's deep structure, we were talking about how good it is to see black men gardening. Neither of us had to say it out loud. We knew.

Our second Japanese maple was more of a bargain, and as it came from a huge hardware/houseware store called Hechinger's, it taught us to always look off the beaten path when buying plants. Twenty-five dollars for the same size maple that easily would have gone for a hundred at a nursery. Again, we struck up conversations surrounding the plant. This time they centered on whether any were left at such prices.

What fun we were having. And what a lasting lesson we were learning: Gardeners love digging in the dirt, yes, but talking about it isn't bad, either.

What a perfect time this would be for Mother to visit, to see me happy, to see me garden, to just be in our space. But it was too late for that. She never got a chance to visit us.

On one occasion, a woman who was renting a room at Mother's home—Shaneetha was her name—telephoned to let us know Mother, who had retired on medical disability from the laundry, had gotten lost while driving. On another, she found Mother passed out on her bedroom floor. Hospitalization and an extensive examination yielded no definitive cause of these episodes, although a doctor did say her electrolytes were out of balance. More medicine, added to the pills she was taking for high blood pressure.

Linda and I knew we were losing her, just at the time we had found each other. Timing again. That awful knowledge was why we began making plans to visit East St. Louis immediately after getting together. Riller and Linda had to meet.

As a world traveler, Linda had seen poverty and squalor, but nothing could have prepared her for East St. Louis in the mid-1980s. Nothing could prepare me, and I had seen it over and over.

Since the good ol' gritty days back in the '50s, when my family first arrived from Mississippi, the city had lost its swagger. By the mid-1980s it was America's worst example of urban decay. The car dealer where I had bought my blue-and-white '56 Ford was no more. In fact the town had no car dealers at all, new or used. And the store where I bought my prom suit, on Collinsville Avenue, downtown, was gone as were many others on that erstwhile bustling street, boarded up, empty. The stockyards where Tootie Fruity had worked were quiet, ghostly, with massive pieces of rusting machinery showing through the decaying walls.

In the neighborhoods, garbage piled up, as many city services lapsed. Residents were hauling their own refuse to dumps, sometimes piling it on rooftops between trips, believing that would prevent rodents from scattering it. They ignored the fact that squirrels and pigeons were right at home up on the roof.

But as bad and sad as the city was, the people, amazingly, persevered in many ways, gardening among them. Arguably, they needed it then more than ever.

In any case, plots I knew from teenhood still grew food. And on our visit, as during each of my trips, my parents' garden gave forth. In East St. Louis, eating, and eating from a garden, was one among few pleasures.

The menu on these homecomings was unfailingly soulful: peas, cornbread, fried fresh corn, fried chicken or pork steaks. And for us lovers of fine cuisine, Mother would prepare the family version of the fatted calf: chitlins. Twenty pounds.

Chitlins were the main ingredient for the feast that Mother had prepared for Linda's visit, believing that there was no better way to meet a woman her son had declared the love of his life.

The chitlins would put the seal of good eating on this final marriage, and in the process, introduce Linda to Mother and to several of her friends.

There was just one problem: Linda had never eaten chitlins, and she had never wanted any. But she was not about to trash chitlins among this group. No way for the new woman in town to act.

After a few drinks around the kitchen table, it was chitlin time.

Plates were heaped high with potato salad, white bread and those delectable hog entrails. I dove in, but a combination of politeness and curiosity caused Mother and her friends to wait and watch Linda before attacking their own plates. Linda carefully twirled some chitlins around her fork, like spaghetti, then picked out a particularly small chit. That perched on her fork, she shook a little hot sauce onto it and added a gob of potato salad. She bit into the bread, then raised the laden fork to her mouth. All chatter and all movement had stopped around the table as Linda withdrew the empty fork.

She chewed. And chewed. Minutes seemed to go by. Finally Mother asked, "How you like 'em, honey?"

Still chewing, Linda kind of shook her head—not quite up and down—and raised her eyebrows. That was enough of a

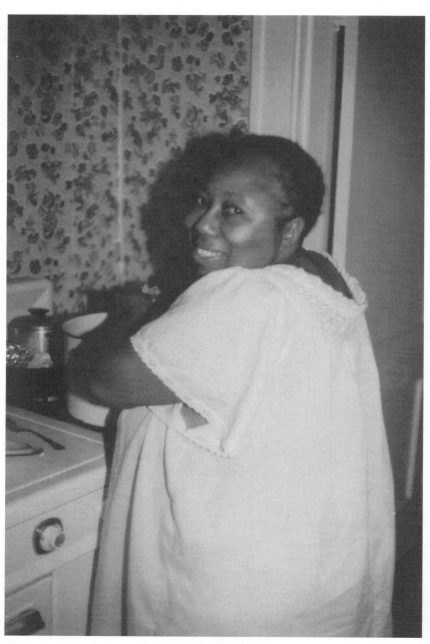

Mother cooking during a visit with Linda and Lee.

signal. The rest of the group put forks and knives to plates in a wonderful eating frenzy. As for Linda, never again would a chit or chitlin pass her lips.

Except for the unfortunate chit experience, the visit was wonderful.

During our first night, a lovely thunderstorm struck the area, blanketing the night with rain, rumbling and flashes of lightning. Nothing in the weather compares with these sights and sounds for evocativeness; they are in some ways like the power and glory and mystery of the sea. Ensconced in the attic space of my mother's home—this one on 37th Street—Linda and I listened to music on a little transistor radio, creating our own blue-lights-in-the-basement party—in the attic, whispering, enjoying ourselves in the dark, laughing with one another. All night long.

Next morning, Mother was already in the kitchen when we staggered down. Standing over a skillet of sausage patties, she greeted us: "How you young 'uns sleep?"

"Great," we said, each hugging Mother in turn.

Breakfast was much more palatable for Linda than dinner had been. Along with the sausage there were grits, scrambled eggs and biscuits. "Anything else you want, hon?" Mother asked Linda.

"No, it all smells and looks wonderful," said Linda, basking in the solicitous motherness—a characteristic as natural to Mother as it was unnatural to Linda's own mother, who instead of nesting at home had had great adventures traveling the world, including a decade-long stay as a State Department employee in Bangladesh.

And, as always, breakfast, dinner or supper, Mother relished seeing people eat themselves into a stupor. We tried.

During our visit—less than a week—we went one day to see one of Mother's friends, Louise, who welcomed us with a panful of barbecued pig snouts, known in East St. Louis as snoots, and a strange and wild song and dance about a "toot toot" or "tutu"—we never determined which. But Louise whirled around her living room floor as the record played, pumping her arms and swaying her hips, while Mother, Linda and I looked on and devoured snoots. Well, two of us devoured.

Our days were filled with such visits and with meandering through the town that I had told Linda so much about. Here's my high school. On this street I used to play touch football. We used to live on this street. And that one. And this one, too.

At night, friends filled the kitchen, eating and drinking much, staying late, then leaving the three of us to one another, to search one another's minds for memories and half-forgotten stories and to listen to one another's hearts tell of the new feelings that we had.

The few days we spent with Mother in East St. Louis were a terribly short time, a relative fragment. But during that briefness, I do believe Mother and Linda confirmed that they were mother and daughter, connected by son and husband, a relationship both of them had always wanted, one they cherished. Linda was the daughter Mother never had, and Riller was the doting mother Linda had never had.

A man is bound to stand by his woman in a case where she and his mother do not get along, assuming of course his woman has not wronged his mother. But no man likes to be in that position of having to make that choice. Thus, I was delighted that the two of them were so clearly soul mates. I was not surprised, as I knew both Linda and my mother to be strong women, self-assured, intelligent, thoughtful, open and open-minded. I loved that in both of them, as I had always loved those qualities in any woman.

They enjoyed what they saw in one another.

Linda and Mother never met again.

Mother's disorientation came back; she would drive some-place, then get lost. We had her hospitalized again. Back at home, she seemed OK for a while, then would pass out again. Electrolytes, repeated the doctor. We can't find any basis for the imbalance; she seems generally in good health. Let's do exploratory surgery, to make sure her lungs are all right. The surgery went fine. Her lungs are healthy. We can't find any basis for the imbalance.

The real deal, of course, was she had just gotten tired of liv-ing without Dad. Medical science couldn't cure that.

It was clear she could no longer drive, so we sold her car, a symbol of the days when we laughed and kidded about whether she would ever learn to drive, a symbol of her inde-pendence. The laughter, the independence, the car were gone.

Through all of this, while I was back and forth between Washington and East St. Louis, my old friend Buch and Sha-neetha, who continued renting the room, were invaluable, calling ambulances, visiting Mother, consulting with me by telephone.

In the late summer of 1986, we reached the point that so many people we'd known had reached before us. Must we put her in a care home? Can we bring her to Washington to live with Linda and me? How could we afford to provide home care for her while we work? We couldn't. A hospital social worker, helping me navigate the guilt, the pain and the defeat that come with such a decision, recommended a care center, just outside East St. Louis. In early September, an ambulance wheeled Mother to the center.

Something deep in her soul must have loved the ride past neat, rolling fields and quiet little homes. But she never talked about it. When I visited her, she did not talk at all. She just lay there, hooked up to wires and a feeding tube. A feeding tube! The mother who could cook up a storm and ate with passion and enjoyment that inspired me for life. A woman so vibrant, so communicative, so in love with life—once—now could not eat. Could not talk.

I talked for both of us, telling stories, catching her up on news about her granddaughters, recalling victims of her lethal home-brewed "tequila," laughing about her laughing with Linda about our romance. From time to time I'd stop and look closely at her face, looking for some sign of recognition. I tried to see the vibrant woman who had sat on the lake shore and expertly tossed her fishing line into the water, her cigarette dangling, the woman who always knew when to scold and when to soothe. No recognition. Nothing. I'd go back to chatting.

When it was time to go, I combed her hair, kissed her cheek and told myself that she smiled. I cried.

Stroke, the doctor said. No extraordinary means, we agreed.

Early on the morning of February 18, 1987, the telephone rang, awakening Linda and me in Washington. It was the call. She had gone at 3:50, someone said. Congestive heart failure.

Is that the medical term for a broken heart?

There was nothing to prepare me for the loss of my mother. Not knowing she had had a stroke and was virtually helpless. Not knowing she had little will to live. Not talking with the doctor, who told it straight. Nothing.

No matter how many times I had seen other people's parents die, no matter how many times I had visualized my own parents' death in my mind, the real nightmare was a jolt. Strange that death seems so shocking, considering its inevitability and how much of it we are shown daily on local television news.

As I had seen other people do, I tried to see her death, and Dad's before hers, as a merciful thing. They're better off now. They aren't suffering any more. They had no quality of life, anyway. And all that was true. But as long as they were alive, there was hope, albeit faint and perhaps irrational, that they would be again what they had been in my youth. Miracles do happen, don't they? Maybe they will at least recover enough to talk and laugh for little spells at a time. Walk around the house a little. Even just sit and rock. But their deaths snuffed out even those tiny hopes.

Thus, I would get no second chance to spend more time with them, to visit more, write more often, telephone more. All those years after I left home and got too busy running the streets and working to make money and trying to make families were years that I was too much out of contact. The importance of being in touch seems to be one of those things too many of us learn too late. Mother and Dad rarely complained about it, and when they did, only gently. Why don't you call us, let us know how you're doing? Write to us sometime. But death, ungently, cruelly, reminds us of what we didn't do and now can't do.

Too, death of a close friend or relative always made me think of my own mortality. My parents' deaths made such thoughts starker. Were there hereditary factors that Mother and I share that helped kill her? How much did our diet, that rich, fat food we loved so much, and the tequila and beer and wine and whisky, how much did that contribute to both their deaths? And the smoking? They wouldn't quit, even after I did and tried to influence them. What about the smoky air in East St. Louis? What about me? And what about my father in Meridian, the other half of that hereditary equation? I wondered, more and more. But I did not get in touch.

In dying at such relatively young ages—Mother at sixty-four, Dad at fifty-eight—my parents missed a lot of good times that surely would have come their way. One, Linda and I felt sure, was our wedding—three months after Mother's death.

We married on May 17 at an airy church of much wood and glass, nestled in the woods of Danvers, Massachusetts, in a ceremony that featured loved ones speaking to and of us and friends and other relatives drawn near. We spoke and cried the ceremony, then laughed and toasted the celebration of it.

Lyn and Lee just married, May 17, 1987, celebrating a champagne life.

Pushing fifty, we marveled that we finally got it right, then marveled some more that we'd been around long enough to have a granddaughter, Lauren Michael, John and Camian's first child, still a babe in arms.

While we were still drying our eyes, we had a laugh when Kay Kirby, a friend from Washington, also struck by my new image as a grandfather, shouted, "Lee, I just can't see you as a grandfather. As a funny uncle, maybe, but not a grandfather."

When it is happy and poignant and teary and jovial, all at the same time, there is something about a beautiful wedding ceremony that somehow intensifies the feeling of love. This one did mine. It was the first time I felt truly committed. It was my last marriage. I couldn't keep doing this.

The certainty I felt about this stemmed largely from my believing that I was in the best of relationships. In Linda I had found a friend, a sister, a lover, a darling, a wife. Strong and independent, yet tender and vulnerable at the same time, she always was able to express concern—say if I was late coming home—without making it seem like distrust. From the beginning I had respected her self-sufficiency, responded to her openness and loved her for both. Most times, a new marriage, even if the couple has lived together, brings a little fear that something will change for the worse, just because of that piece of paper. I had no such worry.

After spending our wedding night at the Parker House, we drove north to Vermont for a week of huge breakfasts, bigger lunches and gargantuan dinners, long walks in the woods and cool nights in a warm room without telephone or television.

We looked back over the previous two years and noted that together we'd survived a bunch of big stress factors—one job change, two moves, two divorces, one death in the immediate family and one marriage. Truly it was cognac time.

When we had squeezed every minute out of our week, we loaded up the rental car and started back to Boston and the airport, stopping along the way on several occasions to gather ferns that I'd spotted along the road. I figured that, although they were New Englanders, they'd get used to living in the brutal summers of the nation's capital.

As soon as we were we back home from our short honeymoon we began planning a longer one—three weeks in Europe in late September, early October. A few days in London, then off to the Isle of Wight, on to France and the rest of the continent. Rail passes, no hotel reservations, no tours.

But first we had some important business to take care of: Linda's name change, which didn't come easy.

"You're the last man I'll change my name for," she told me.

On one level that declaration was flattering, but I knew that what she really meant was: nevermore. No more new Social Security card, no more new bank card, driver's license, no more new stationery.

And, most important, no more loss of identity that comes with losing your last name.

This would be her second change. Born Linda Marie Dandridge, she married David Harris and became Linda Harris, remaining so for all her professional and more than half her personal life. Then I came along with yet another name.

Linda decided to take it, despite the growing practice among women not to make the change and despite the fact that she was losing her professional name.

While Linda Harris sounded just fine, Linda May simply would not do, we reasoned. We could hear the smirky questions: "Linda Mae what?" Nor would using her middle name work. Linda Marie May just didn't have the ring she wanted.

The answer: Lyn May. With a last name like May, you need a first name with either one syllable or three. Two sound funny. So Linda's first name became Lyn. Sounded right. And we could live with the questions about whether we made up Lee and Lyn, as the two did have a certain symmetry that we liked.

Taking the multi-step approach, she first became Linda

Harris May, then, ever so briefly, Linda May, before finally becoming Lyn May. Throughout the process, which took about a year, we both had to come to terms with some hard emotions.

While Lyn had to choose whether to jettison a name she'd had for a quarter-century, I had to deal with why I thought she should. Certainly, part of my reasoning was the hope that our having the same last name would symbolize our sharing emotions and attitudes that, in turn, would make a happy life.

At the same time, I knew that part of my motivation centered on another symbolic matter: my desire for a fresh start that a name change can signal. And, yes, there were times when I wondered, as any man must, whether my reason had anything to do with wanting to wipe out this remnant of my wife's past life. Some, I concluded.

So, as she lamented the prospect of her loss, I pulled for it, a sure way to get into weird, philosophical debates. Changing your name can be freeing, I argued, citing my own change in graduate school, where I dropped Eddie.

"That wasn't your last name," was my love's retort.

"But Harris wasn't always your last name," I said.

"But it's the one I had the longest," she said. And so it went.

Happily, the change took. Her last. She was as clear about that as I was about her being my last wife.

All squared away on the name thing, we refocused on our autumn vacation/honeymoon. Amazingly, it worked just as we had planned it. We alternated between big cities and small towns, staying until we were ready to move on. As we both loved food, we sometimes planned entire trips around a single meal. Mussels were such a case. Having found a wonderful lunch of them in Oostende, Belgium, we were told by the server that the Netherlands had the absolute best in Europe.

Well, what luck. We'd be going to Amsterdam soon. But

first, the little town in Germany, Schwelm, where as a boy soldier I had spent so much good time. I had to show it to Lyn.

I had to show her a part of my growing up. I wanted her to know more than was possible with our meeting so late in life.

I could not have explained that to the people we ran into at a little restaurant in Dusseldorf the night before we went to Schwelm. An Italian restaurant, run by a mysterious Romanian.

After we were there for a few minutes everybody started talking at us, from various corners of the room.

"So, where will you go next?" asked a German woman.

"Schwelm," Lyn and I said.

"Schwelm!?" the young woman exclaimed, incredulously. "That's a cow town."

Goat, actually, as a herd of goats was what we saw on a hill, just outside of town. The taxi driver stopped, and we all communed. The young woman in the restaurant couldn't have stood it.

Like Lyn, I was, in some ways, seeing Schwelm for the first time, too. I could not tell how much the little town had changed. I did know that I was intensely more interested in what folks were growing in their yards and window boxes than I had been twenty-six years earlier (hydrangeas and geraniums). And we spent hours in a quiet museum on a hill, one filled with every manner of clock imaginable. At the lovely inn where we stayed, I discovered that I had not lost my love for schnitzel, which we had in abundance, along with local beer for me and wine for Lyn. Alas, I saw none of that old poetry-reading, wine-drinking, jazz-playing gang of mine.

In the same way I had wanted Lyn to see Schwelm, I wanted her to see Amsterdam's business girls in the windows, perhaps daughters of those who years ago had enticed a young man from East St. Louis. We saw them, and they were wary, hostile even as we walked down the sidewalk, as they knew a man and woman could only be there to look, not to buy. How changed I was since my last walk through that district.

My last time in Holland, I never would have spent a day looking for the perfect mussels. But Lyn and I did, hopping a train, heading north, getting off in a little town we'd never heard of. One restaurant was open. It had mussels, and, yes, they were the best we'd ever had. The weather, no doubt, helped, a perfect mussel day, drizzly, gray, slightly raw. We loved it.

But not quite as much as we loved the Isle of Wight. We were entranced by the fact we could walk the entire island, north to south, by the pubs along the way and by the gorgeous hydrangeas whose leaves had turned a mellow burgundy and gold. We wandered upon a nursery one day, and the owner, who recognized a kindred spirit despite differences of color and nationality, toured us, showing us a few familiar plants but many more that were totally new to us.

Nevertheless, we talked for a long time, swapping stories of success and failure and beauty and peace in the garden, proving again that gardening, like love, food and music, speaks a universal language.

Having come from Washington, where people seemed numb to murder and rape and burglary (we were welcomed with a break-in a few months after moving in), we reveled in sitting quietly in a pub where the greatest excitement had to do with somebody's fishing boat springing a leak. It was in a pub one night that a woman heard me say I had forgotten to pack a book, then lent me one of John Mortimer's Rumpole volumes. Quickly, I grew to love the wily, claret-loving barrister and long-suffering spouse of She Who Must Be Obeyed.

And to walk along a path, see a man thatching a roof and talk with him about his craft for half an hour, as we did one day, was like being in another world. It was another world.

But even there, dread apparently lives. One day we overheard a young boy, about nine or ten say, inexplicably, to his adult companion as they walked on a pier, heading to shore, "Better safe than sorry." What could he have been talking about? What could make him either safe or sorry at such a wonderfully carefree age? Or is youth endangered in some way everywhere, even if not by Uzis?

So sad, a youth that likely never will be spent.

Hearing the youngster's admonition, Lyn and I laughed, then vowed to redouble our efforts to keep enough of our own youth to spend recklessly.

Back in the U.S.A., we discovered we were missing about half the dozen or so rolls of film we shot, including those of Paris, the Isle of Wight, Wales, Brugge. After the initial disappointment, we were OK, realizing that we had far better pictures in our heads and in our hearts.

In addition to the images of Notre Dame and such, we carried one that centered on the common European practice of speaking to people on entering a restaurant, something we rarely saw in America. That resonated with me, perhaps because it seemed familiarly Southern. But on another level, it seemed practical. I believe that making a connection with another person, through speaking, looking into his face, makes it more difficult for that person to knock you in the head, steal your money, shoot you.

Inspired, I tried speaking to people in eateries, on streets, even in (gasp) elevators. Many were responsive, while others seemed uncomfortable. Saddest were the dead-eyed young men who did not speak back. Not because they were "igging" me, as my mother would have said, but because they were too drugged to comprehend.

Around our home, the year 1988 is remembered mostly as the year Lyn and I became cat people.

Having grown up with Pup Pup and Snowball, I was a dog man from way back. And, of course, my friends the Michaels had declared me Caninus Emeritus, insuring that my dog heritage would be duly noted.

But things change. A friend who was going out of town asked us to cat sit for her. We did and got to like the little boy. It was my first extended exposure to a feline, although Lyn had cared for her daughter's cat. She was not impressed, however, declaring that cat boring.

So we both were surprised that we took to the little cat. As it was near Lyn's birthday in August, I suggested that a cat be her gift. OK, she said, hesitantly.

The day before her birthday we cruised a huge cat show in Virginia, impressed by some of the spectacular specimens on display but intimidated at their prices. Over at the D.C. animal shelter on Georgia Avenue, we found looks we liked and prices we could afford. Lyn settled on a tortoiseshell, and we voiced her choice to the shelter folks.

Fine, they said, but first the Cat Lady has to check out our home. They didn't call her the Cat Lady, but that's what she was. So the next day, the Cat Lady pulled up in front of our house on her bicycle, wearing Sunday finery, including a nice wide-brimmed sun hat.

Inside, she sat primly on the edge of a chair, facing the two of us as we sat on the edge of the sofa. Also in on the interview was my eldest daughter, who by this time had become a comfortable and important part of our lives.

"If you are granted a cat, will you declaw it?" she asked.

Fortunately, we had read the literature we got from the cat show. "Noooo," we said together.

"Will this cat be an indoor cat, or an outdoor cat?"

"Indoor," we chorused.

Having failed to trick us with this line of questioning, the Cat Lady tried a trump card. "I see you're only getting one cat. You should get two."

She almost got us to give up on getting the cat, as we considered it a stretch to get just one. Unperturbed, she argued ahead, telling us two cats would keep each other company and be no more trouble and little more expense than a single cat.

She failed to intimidate us. We agreed on two females, the tortoiseshell, who we named Vincent Marie, and a calico, who became Calvin Lee. The Cat Lady was right; they weren't much trouble. And I guess they do keep each other company, after a fashion. Hissing and moaning at each other, boxing for turf and glaring at each other as if they're from different planets whenever one enters the room.

They went through a serious period of adjustment to the house plants, chewing anything that reminded them of grass, such as spider plants and palms. I tried putting Tabasco and cayenne pepper on the leaves, to no effect. I tried putting orange peels on top of the soil, having heard that cats do not like the smell of citrus. Once or twice I tried squirting them with water, but that seemed cruel.

It was not until years later that I noticed both cats liked nibbling on bamboo during their infrequent ventures outside. I began growing dwarf bamboo inside, placing pots strategically around the house. They loved it and left the other plants alone. The secret was, I never let them know the bamboo was theirs.

Their eccentricities aside, Calvin and Vincent are marvelous. "My best birthday gift," Lyn said, asserting that they really do love each other and that if one disappeared the other would miss her. Yes, Cats That Love.

They have been my gift, too, a gift of learning. They have taught me lessons about patience and persistence, both of which they possess in abundance. Into my lap they'll jump a hundred times until I give in. Or they'll wait for days at a window to see their favorite car go by, or whatever it is they wait there for.

Knowing when to say no is a terrific lesson they've taught. No, I don't want you to rub me now. I have to take a nap, another nap. Such independence appeals to me. In a cat and in a woman. I was a cat man all along.

* * *

After eight years in Washington, I was about to find out why so many journalists wanted to cover the White House. Having written about immigration issues for the past several years, I was getting a change of pace in covering President Reagan for part of his last year in office.

Much of that time was campaign time, as Reagan stumped his way back and forth across the country. He was campaigning not just for George Bush, of course, but for his own legacy.

Months of watching him close up showed me that he was more than an affable dunce. He had a knack for touching buttons in audiences that made them truly believe he was looking out for their interests, fighting off the liberal bad guys who were bent on destroying a wonderful life. Reagan, who appealed to older people as a peer and to surprisingly young ones as maybe a grandfather, could deliver a hokey line and make it feel genuine.

Once, in Texas, he closed a speech, saying something about riding off into the sunset. And a few moments later, the president of the United States actually climbed onto a buckboard and rode out of the arena. The crowd loved it, just as a California audience loved his delivery of a line urging voters to stand by Bush—and "stand by me," complete with a catch in his voice.

All of this made him a great communicator, but it did not make him a great president.

On the contrary, Reagan's policies, including appointing masses of socially conservative federal judges, undermining efforts to correct past racial injustice and weakening federal environmental laws, did serious damage to the nation's people. And on an emotional level, his policies and the attitudes and behavior of his administration officials fostered a climate of polarization among races and economic classes.

But was he a nice man, personally?

He certainly seemed warm and friendly. And he and Nancy seemed to show genuine affection for each other. But it is impossible to separate a man's policies from his personality.

Reagan and any other president aside, covering the White House was in some ways pampered duty, as every utterance of the President was tape-recorded and transcribed by a corps of transcriptionists and handed out to the boys and girls, post haste. In other ways, the job was brutal, with endless travel and, like the Army, a great deal of hurrying up and waiting. Incumbent White House correspondents like Julie Johnson, then of the *New York Times*, helped make these dead spots come alive, as we talked about family, flowers and other delights back home.

Times had changed for me: travel no longer was a welcome escape from home. My garden no longer was a bag vase in my garment bag; it was in my yard. And my heart and soul were at home. But going away still was part of the job.

My White House stint ended in January 1989, when Reagan handed over power to George Bush, the man who had stood by him. Following the inauguration, Ron, Nancy and a few of us boys and girls boarded an Air Force jet and flew off to California, toward the sunset.

It was a low-key happy trip. The former first couple mingled like congenial hosts, standing in the aisle of the plane (no longer Air Force One because Reagan was no longer president), sharing champagne and chat with their fellow travelers, who casually took notes. It seemed surreal that one minute a man could be the Leader of the Free World, then the next minute he is Ordinary Man, going to meet the moving van. The transfer of presidential power is so orderly, it's scary, as if nothing really changes from one leader to the next. In some ways, nothing did that year.

By the time we got to 1989, Lyn and I had built a life in Washington that had real routines, including going to the Safeway (Washington was the only city we'd ever seen a grocery store—the Georgetown Safeway—famous for sightings of diplomats and senators), movie theaters and restaurants. Living in D.C. was feeling just like living in a real city, not simply the home of the federal government.

Because it was the home of the federal government, we found it incongruous that the city never seemed integrated socially, despite its large numbers of affluent minorities. Expense-account restaurants on K Street, museums, even black-oriented plays at the Kennedy Center all were attended by audiences that made the city look like it was Vanilla City instead of Chocolate City.

So curious was I that I did a story for the *Times*, asking black people why they did not go to such places. Disappointingly, many said they simply did not feel comfortable. I did not understand that kind of discomfort, as many of those saying they did not feel comfortable had never been barred from going anywhere because of color, never had been forced to drink at a water fountain for colored only.

Also sad was the fear that some black people expressed about being thought of as "bourgie" if they were caught at cultural events like the symphony or Shakespearean plays at the Folger.

Cynthia Lewis, a good friend of ours, had the best explanation for such mind gyrations involving race: "Being black is really complicated."

Being black also was an asset on certain stories. In race coverage, some black people open up more to a black writer. That is one of the reasons that, when news organizations began hiring black writers, most of them were assigned to the race beat or the civil rights beat or the urban affairs beat, all ways of describing what some black reporters eventually began to disparage as "the chitlin beat."

I love chitlins, but I have always resented seeing black writers asked to cover simple black stories only because of color— stories such as a report finding that minorities were discriminated against. No special understanding, no historical experience was necessary to regurgitate numbers and conclusions in a story like that. One about welfare rolls increasing would be offensive for the same reason, and doubly offensive because assigning it to "the black writer" implies that welfare is a black thing. I resented such assignments for myself and for others, even though I knew some black writers actually sought such assignments. My feeling was that accepting race assignments without sifting through them amounted to journalistic segregation.

The race factor played parts in some of my assignments, and that was OK, as editors and I talked them out, sometimes deciding that I would do the stories and sometimes not.

Unfortunately, no amount of talking with editors or writers has stopped the wrongheaded practice of calling any black person heading an organization or business or holding public office a "black leader" and the condescending reference to "the black community" as if we all lived and thought in the same village. Both reflect some primitive journalistic need to homogenize.

When the commemoration of the twenty-fifth anniversary of the murders of civil rights workers James Chaney, Michael Schwerner and Andrew Goodman was approaching, the *Los Angeles Times* wanted to be there. However, as Atlanta bureau chief David Treadwell was busy elsewhere, editors asked if I could do it.

An easy decision to make. Good story. And, ironically, it came just after I had been offered the assignment of heading the Atlanta bureau. David was transferring to New York.

Would I want to go back to Atlanta?

Would Lyn want to go to Atlanta?

Yes.

Our discussion did not take long. That was becoming a pattern with us. We hated kvetching. We laid out the pros and cons (actually, selling our home in a falling real estate market was the only con) and made the decision.

Having done so, we began missing what we would miss about Washington.

The museums were incomparable, and you couldn't beat the prices. We'd miss walking down the hill to the National Gallery, where cherry blossoms danced like snow along the building's walls. And we'd miss flying into National Airport at night, when the lit monuments were so spectacular that we truly believed democracy was a beautiful thing—not that it was like sausage, whose manufacture should never be seen by those who love it.

Ethiopian restaurants, Vietnamese restaurants, the Botanic Garden, the Arboretum, food shopping at Eastern Market, Sunday drives through the Virginia countryside—we'd miss them all. And friends.

And so, change was in the air when I dialed my father's number to tell him I'd be covering the story in Philadelphia, Mississippi, near his home in Meridian.

Not knowing the number by heart, I had to look it up. That called attention to our unfamiliarity, the gulf between us. Amazing how strange it feels to have to call information to get the telephone number for your father, who might be dead for all you know. With each digit that I punched, I wondered, Should I stop here? Do I really want to make this call? What happens when he answers? What if he doesn't? What if his wife answers? How can you leave a message that says hello and that you decided to ring up your father after almost forty years?

By the time I had hit the last number, I was resolved. No matter who answered, it would be OK. The telephone wire would be an intermediary, a buffer. For him and for me. It wasn't like just showing up on his doorstep. Talking, if only briefly, would give us both a chance to get used to this strange notion of contact. At the same time, I hoped it would allow me to gauge his attitude, hear something in his voice that would tell me I was, indeed, doing the right thing.

I had been in Mississippi, even in Meridian, on other assignments over the years, but I had not gotten in touch, even though I thought about it each time I visited the state. This was the right time. I was middle-aged, he was old, putting us at ages when we ought to be reconciling differences in our lives—and indifferences. In our case, it was indifferences. Neither of us had sought out the other, and I had not regretted that because my other parents had been so loving and caring. Now, I was, essentially, an orphan. And he was short a son. In proposing that we meet, I was aiming to change both situations before it was too late.

"I figured this would be a good chance to drop by and see you," I said into the telephone.

"Yeah, yeah, come on by," he said in a tone so easy and familiar that it easily leaped across the nearly forty years that lay between us. I would arrive in Meridian on the afternoon of June 20, rent a car and drive to his home.

When that day came, I started my trip chores early in the morning, as usual, watering all the plants outside, then the ones inside, grooming as I went. Lyn always feared watering, believing she would drown something. Or maybe she only said that because she knew I needed to do it.

I always made watering a long, slow process, hours long. Partly because there were so many plants, but also because it was more than watering. It was a somber farewell. Even if I planned to be away only for a day or so, I knew much change could take place. I would touch each plant as I watered it, checking its health and making a mental photograph of its size, color, shape. Then I could make comparisons on the happy day I returned.

The watering done, I thought about whether I should take my father something, a gift, maybe, or photographs. But what do you give a man you do not know? And what pictures would be meaningful to him from thirty-nine years of my life, the life of a stranger? I decided not to take anything.

I just went.

After the long, fearsome walk down that little familiar, strange sidewalk, after our talk and walk in my father's garden, after I realized that I had done the right thing in coming, after all that, I could begin to concentrate on the story I had come to cover.

Back in Mississippi. Back where I'd lived thirty-four years earlier, where I'd left soon after Emmett Till was kidnapped and murdered in 1955. And now I was back to write about one of his many ghosts, three other murders that took place on June 21, 1964, echoing the anger and hate and violence that raged through this and other states of the Deep South.

As part of their efforts to register black voters, Chaney, a black twenty-one-year-old Meridianite, and white New Yorkers, Schwerner, twenty-four, and Goodman, twenty, visited a black church that had been burned by Klansmen. After they left, the black civil rights worker and his two colleagues were arrested on speeding charges by the Neshoba County sheriff. The three were released about 10:30 p.m. after Chaney paid a $20 fine.

They were reported missing the next day, prompting the county sheriff to speculate that they had "hid out somewhere, trying to get a lot of publicity, I figure." Their bullet-ridden bodies were found forty-four days later, buried in an earthen dam five miles from Philadelphia.

Mississippi dropped murder charges involving nineteen white men—local law enforcement officials and members of the Ku Klux Klan—but the men were tried on civil rights charges in federal court. Seven were convicted, one pleaded guilty, eight were acquitted and the cases of three ended in mistrials.

(In the Till case, two white men were acquitted by an all-white jury.)

Recalling the murders and the times was chilling for the busloads of people—black and white—who had gathered at the spot on this desert-hot day. "I get goose bumps knowing that people could be so mean to take a person's life like that," a woman from Philadelphia, Pennsylvania, told me. "It's too much, just too much."

For me, it was especially chilling, as Chaney and I had lived in the same town, were the same color, close to the same age. Like Till, he could have been me.

Mississippi was one of the nine Southeastern states I was inheriting as the incoming Southern bureau chief for the *Times.* I could only hope there would not be many such commemorations. While I appreciate history and our need to know it—good and bad—I didn't want to encounter too many ghosts or feel too many chills from Jim Crow's past.

At home in the District of Columbia, it was a time for goodbyes and for packing.

The goodbyes were long, tough and tender, including a bureau fete of sushi and several home-cooked meals at friends, including one at Paul Houston's during which we laughed about our chitlin meals with Mother, recounted the years that we'd all spent on the Potomac and unveiled the hopes that Lyn and I had for our new life together in the New South.

Having moved so many times, I felt that after this one I did not have any more moves left. I was hoping it was like marriage—my last.

Packing seemed a simple enough matter, as the newspaper was footing the packing and moving bill. But nooooo. When I told the moving folks I wanted to move all the potted plants, indoors and outdoors, they balked.

"You'll have to get a permit from the Agriculture Department, certifying that your plants don't have any diseases," said a moving company official. "You have to do that to cross state lines."

The man probably thought the notion of dealing with the

federal bureaucrats would intimidate me. He didn't know that I dealt with bureaucrats for a living. Nor did he know the pull that a person's plants can have. No way was I going to give up plants I had known from their infancy.

There was, of course, Sarah Frond, quite zaftig by now, dominating any space she occupied. There was the orange tree, started from a seed that I stuck in an eighteen-inch pot one day during dinner, ignoring the experts' warning against "overpotting," reasoning that if the tree can grow in the ground as big as it is, surely it can grow in a pot, no matter what the size. The growing collection of African violets certainly had to go to Georgia.

And, outside, I wasn't going to leave my half-barrels with the Japanese maples, along with all the other friends I had grown and known for four years now.

Get approval from the Ag Department? Sure, I told the moving man. I telephoned and explained my situation to an Ag official.

"Are your plants free of disease?" the man asked.

"Yes," I answered.

"All right, we'll send you a certification form to sign," he said. He did, I did, all was properly documented.

When I presented the form to the moving man, I could swear I saw disappointment in his eyes. Not surprising. It took three grown men an entire eight-hour shift just to pack the plants.

But what a great job they did, giving me confidence that I could send any plant anywhere, anytime. One by one, they watered a plant, then wrapped its pot with damp newspaper and put the whole thing in a box padded with dry newspaper. This process was repeated with each of the dozens and dozens of pots.

No problem for Lyn and me on that end. But in Atlanta five days later, we were the unpackers. And it was July in Georgia.

SECOND TIME AROUND

I hit the ground gardening.

I had a shovel in my hand even as the movers unloaded the boxes from the van. Anxious to free the cooped-up plants as quickly as possible, we'd rip open the cartons and snatch the pots out, placing some on the porch and on a passageway along the side of the house. Others I planted in the ground immediately, including the two Japanese maples.

In those first days, friends Schuyler and Diana Rector helped feed my frenzy to cover all the ground in our yard by contributing perennial plants from their lovely garden, including loads of ajuga, strawberry geranium and hosta. Quickly I established relationships with local nurserymen, buying dozens of shrubs and trees—never mind that it was the hottest time of the year, and I should wait until fall to plant; patience is not always there for a gardener—even for one with cats, who are the models of patient living. So intent was I on immediately filling in all the spaces, I planted a house plant, China doll, thinking it would maybe last until the first frost. To my surprise, it returned the next spring, and each one thereafter. That was a graphic example of why it pays to push limits—in gardening as in life.

My rush to grow as much as possible as soon as possible was like my relationship with Lyn. We were in our forties when we met, so we felt we had to live fast and catch up on fun we'd missed together, step up our pleasure in life and each other. And in a sense, my father and I had done that too, in that first meeting, quickly, naturally finding a relationship by narrowly focusing on our common love of gardening.

When I came up for air after my initial dive into planting in Atlanta, I began to have second thoughts about the size of the gardening space.

Having been boxed in so quickly by the tiny space in Washington, anything bigger than a breadbox would seem expansive. So when we decided on our two-story Victorian, built in 1890, I did not worry about the size of the ground space, slightly wider than the house and about the depth of the street in our West End neighborhood. Soon, however, I began thinking that, not only was I going to finally realize my long-time wish to fill in my entire yard with plants, no grass, but that I was maybe going to need more space to satisfy my gardening needs. I put these thoughts on hold, and, fortunately, eventually concluded the space was right.

Living with it helped: just watching what happened with the light and the shadows, how existing plants made me feel when I walked through the gates in the front and in back. And just as we undid some of the previous owners' decorating inside the house—replacing sconces and heavy curtains with shutters to allow in more light, removing carpeting to see the heart pine floors—I undid some of the plantings, beginning with the removal of boxwoods lining the back wall and azaleas lining a wrought-iron fence in the front. Some of the azaleas found homes with Sky and Di. This done, the space seemed to grow dramatically, just as the house had seemed to become more open and spacious.

Meanwhile, I had to pay attention to my outside job with the *Times*. And in my early months back in Atlanta, it interfered dramatically with my gardening.

As Atlanta bureau chief, I was chief of myself and Edith Stanley, researcher and, along with her husband, Frank, an avid gardener. Chiefing meant writing news and features from the nine southeastern states.

And that meant I got to chase all the tragedies in the region that I and the editors back in Los Angeles thought were worthy of being reported in our pages. As fate would have it, my first five months in the region were a very busy news period. The trial of the Rev. Jim Bakker, convicted of bilking his believers, caused me to take up part-time residence in Charlotte, North Carolina, while Hurricane Hugo had me virtually parachuting into the Virgin Islands and Charleston, South Carolina, to cover the pain and destruction. The mail-bomb murder of a federal judge in Birmingham, Alabama, a killer tornado in Huntsville, Alabama, and the long, strange court case involving frozen embryos in Tennessee all kept me hopping.

As Tom McCarthy, a buddy from the *Times'* Washington bureau, put it, "Lee, you took what had been a features beat and turned it into CNN."

"Self-defense," I assured him, "self-defense." Because by that time, hitting the road the way I used to in the old days in Washington was beginning to get old. Lyn, home and the garden were exerting a powerful pull.

Of course, national newspaper correspondents are nothing if not Pavlovian; so, time after time, friends from other papers and I would converge on some bad news spot when the bell rang. And between tragedies, we'd stick notebooks in our pockets and strike out to ferret out features, always searching for one that would make Page One.

Between trips, I enjoyed seeing what changes time had brought Atlanta. And introducing it to Lyn, who had spent only short times in the city, was a treat for me. I loved many of the changes, sensing that both architecture and cuisine had improved greatly since I had lived in the city during the 1970s. Then, glass phallic symbols symbolized the city's cutting edge in building design, and going out for an exotic meal meant snaring a thick-crust pizza.

This time around we found delight in several new buildings, each of which had wonderfully whimsical tops, including those looking like two bear heads, the Brooklyn Bridge, the Chrysler Building.

And, demonstrating the city's growing immigrant population, we ate ourselves around the globe in restaurants serving Vietnamese, Thai, Ethiopian and other foods.

As the restaurants suggested, Georgians, like people throughout the region, were, for the first time, having to deal with varied ethnic relations in the same way as people in cities like New York, Boston, Chicago and Los Angeles: no longer were black Americans and white Americans the only ethnic groups around. In one of my regular sushi bars, I saw just how truly worldly the city was becoming: a black man and white man were being seated by a Filipino maitre d' and served sushi by a Laotian chef. This was the new Georgia. We liked it.

But stories kept calling, so I was on the road again. The good news was that I saw more of the South than most folks ever do (or want to) and met a lot of people who were truly delightful and interesting. The bad news was the unpredictability of these trips—and the fact that so many of them focused on tragedy or anger or discord, totally alien to my personal life.

Thus, I was beginning to wear out my knees parachuting into those little towns looking for quote. I began asking, in journalism, is this all there is?

To help make my road wars more meaningful, I began shopping for the garden whenever possible. Driving a rental car from home usually worked better logistically than flying and then renting a car, so I would often meander back to Atlanta, stopping at nurseries off the well-driven path and filling the car trunk with mementos of my personal road wars.

Every gardener has gathered plants that evoke memories of a time or place or person, and these certainly did that. But they also would recall part of a career, softening the hard parts in retrospect years after I no longer would be out there.

In early 1990, I picked up a native azalea in Fairhope, Alabama, on the way back from Biloxi, Mississippi, whose growing beauty and fragrant orange blossoms would mingle with my memory of interviewing all day and writing all night about the Vietnamese shrimpers and how their hostile welcome to the Gulf Coast had changed to respect from the native-born Americans.

And the hulking yucca blooming with prickly elegance would remind me not only of Hampton, the little South Carolina town divided over its stinking medical waste incinerator, but also of the conversation I had with the nursery owner about the joy of walking in rain—the light, cool kind that was falling on the day I bought the little yucca from him. It all recalled the day I stripped naked and showered in the downpour in Germany so many years before.

One of my more interesting road collections came from Gadsden, Alabama, where I had gone to report a story about the town's economic health. Toward evening, rain was pouring on my rental car but not enough to obscure the prickly pear cactus that stood at the gate of a little run-down shotgun house like a twisted two-foot-tall, needled monument—beckoning me.

I screeched to a halt, giving in to an urge I had had often as I screamed down back roads throughout the South and admired the casually growing cactus with its blooms as yellow and cheerful as a pansy's.

Knock, knock.

"Who's there?"

"Lee May."

"Who?"

"Lee May. A reporter."

Eventually, a man, about sixty years old, scowled his way to the door and growled: "Whaddya want?"

"A piece of that cactus," I said, getting right to the point, then explaining what a beautiful thing I thought it was and how much I had always wanted one of these old-fashioned plants and what beautiful blooms it would have and how if he would just give me some newspaper to protect my hands, a butcher knife to cut it and a plastic bag to carry it in, I'd take a cutting that wouldn't hurt the plant at all.

"It ain't mine. Belongs to my girlfriend," the man explained.

Oh, well, I'm sure she wouldn't mind if I just took a little whack off it, I said. After a bit of soul-searching, he agreed, bringing me my tools. That was the best part of the trip.

At home, carpenters, electricians, plumbers and other crafts-men were working steadily to give us a bigger kitchen, a big-ger upstairs bathroom, a couple of tile floors, a wall of book-cases, a new ceiling, a new pine floor and a wall of block glass where one small window had been. For six months, we lived through knocked-down walls, holes in the floor, dust in the air and tension, too. But we survived it and came away believing that if our marriage could get through the renovation wars, it could get through anything.

As one of our many celebrations of the end of renovation in the spring of 1990, Lyn and I decided to drive to Mississippi to see my father. She had not met him and I was looking for-ward to seeing him again. We'd only talked by telephone since my initial visit.

On a sunny Saturday afternoon, Lyn and I climbed into our dusty 1986 Honda Prelude and set off on I-20 West, relishing the drive, as being on the road together is one of our pastimes. Not that it ranks as high as eating.

Eating, like gardening, always has been an important fixture in my life and in my relationships. It is a social lubricant, more universal than drinking, and certainly more varied in its sensu-ality. A whole range of textures, tastes, smells, sights and even sounds go with the food experience, its rich variety recalling a well-developed perennial and annual garden at its peak.

In one of our early eating adventures, Lyn and I pigged out on sushi. While I don't smoke, a sushi orgy always makes me want a cigarette. It was her first time. That was before chitlins and happily, different. Later, discovering the depth of my love for raw fish and rice, Lyn said, "It's a good thing I loved sushi; I have a feeling that if I hadn't, I never would have seen you again."

Some of our past food ventures were on our minds as we motored west.

Lyn and I have cried and laughed from time to time about our visit to Mother's, scene of the chitlin caper.

I asked Lyn if she actually swallowed the little chit, thinking she may have somehow extracted it and left it on her plate. "Of course I swallowed it," she said, frowning as if she could see the plate again. "What did you think I did with it?"

"Well, how was it?"

"Rubbery."

"No, not the texture, the taste. How did it taste?"

"Rubbery."

Then, somewhere around Anniston, she wondered, aloud, "Mary and your father won't have any chitterlings, will they?"

"Chitlins, not chitterlings," I said. "No, I don't think they'll have any. But if they do, pull a Nancy Reagan; just say no. I'll eat your part."

Fears of deja vu jumped on her, anyway. She probably had visions of a giant chitlin squirming and wiggling, wrapping itself around her face, forcing itself into her mouth.

"What do you think they'll have?"

"Something outta the garden. Some kinda fried meat."

"Yum."

Lyn, born in Canton, Ohio and raised in Columbus, Ohio, hadn't begun to love fried food quite the way I always had, but in other ways she was getting to be a pretty decent Southern eater, loving cornbread, biscuits and grits. Although she still preferred hash browns. And, I had some work to do in teach-

ing her that the stuff piled around the turkey is called dressing, not stuffing.

Nonetheless, her concern about what we were going to be
fed during our visit demonstrated a Southern trait. What's to
be eaten seems not as big a deal for most Northerners. In fact,
many Southerners argue that Northerners don't feed guests
anything at all.

Southerners I've known used to joke that if you go to a
Northerner's home, you always got offered a drink. Right
away. Go to a Southerner's home, and it was food you got
offered—and drink as well, of course.

Lyn and I had left the subject of food by the time we made
Birmingham, which takes an eternity to drive through on I-20.
We turned our talk to my earlier visit the year before and what
this one was likely to bring. There was no way to know, of
course, but my father and I had had telephone conversations
that were as warm as could be.

Twenty miles before Meridian, there is Cuba, Alabama, my
birthplace. Like many people, Lyn was amused to see a road
sign announcing it, as the town is barely a bump in the road.
Her amusement gave way to delight as we slowly drove
through the quiet streets and admired the old white houses
with the fern-laden porches.

As in small towns and along back roads throughout the
South, practically every person we saw greeted us with the
stares always directed at strangers and with a wave. People sitting on porches or walking along the road raise the entire hand,
while most drivers lift a single finger from the steering wheel
(no, the index finger, not the one that many city drivers raise).

In town, the little mercantile store, like so many in rural
areas across America, was dark and empty. And, as in tiny
towns throughout the nation, drugs and the crime they inspire
plague the good people. "Yes, there's crack here, just like in the
big cities," a woman told me sadly.

The log cabin I was born in was away from town, up in the

little hills and had long ago been swallowed up by vines and trees and pulled down by those mighty plants and by time.

Like seeing my father after so many years, being back in Cuba after a decades-long absence brought back boxes of memories I rarely opened.

This was the home of the little white Baptist church where I was baptized in the mid-1940s, where I would hang out with my Uncle Buddy and his friends during the day-long Sunday services. Standing barely past his knees, I would walk big as I followed Buddy and his buddies down through the woods where they would take their midday break. Always they would talk and laugh. And they would scratch around in the leaves around a big tree and uncover a pint bottle of brown liquid—which they would pass around, each man taking a swig. Despite this transgression, maybe the preaching did these men good; I never knew of any of them going out like a crack-crazed addict and knocking anyone on the head.

On this visit, Lyn began her own relationship with Cuba, and from then on, stopping in the little town became part of our going-to-Meridian ritual.

It was daytime when we passed Club Ala. Miss., and daylight cast the place in a harsh light, the way morning too often portrays a seemingly charming date picked up at a bar just before closing time. The night time is the right time for a juke joint, and we agreed to check out Club Ala. Miss. some night, if it is still kicking.

Meridian, too, looked harsh, as we entered a grimy side of town, a gathering of industrial buildings, and wound our way through downtown, eventually hitting 30th Avenue, my father's street. On the way to his house, I was struck by the splendor of several Victorian homes, having taken no note of them when I was growing up.

At my father's home, the sidewalk did not seem nearly as long as before.

He sat on the porch, easing into a slow smile as we approached. Mary appeared, and I introduced Lyn to them.

"I've heard a lot about you," Lyn said to my father.

"Yeah. Well, some of it's probably true," he said, grinning. "You know you have to always be careful 'bout believin' what you hear 'bout somebody."

Sensing that he was about to get wound up, Mary stepped in. "I know y'all hungry. Come on in here and eat. They hungry, Ples. Don't start talkin' now."

"I'm jus' tellin' the truth," he said.

To the kitchen table we went, where I was directed to sit at the head, while Lyn was admonished for even thinking about sitting there. "That's the man's place," said Mary.

As we came to learn was her custom, Mary, like so many Southern women of the past, did not join us in the meal. Instead, she sat in a chair away from the table, chatted for a while before retiring to the porch. At first we wondered about this ("I already ate," she said), but like so much in any family's behavior we came to accept it with no wonder and with no real explanation needed.

My father did eat with us. Peas, from the garden, as I had eaten on my visit the year before. And cornbread, with boiled okra, tomato slices and a plate of fried pork steaks. Heaven for me. And for Lyn, at least it wasn't chitlins.

It was a comfortable visit. The only awkwardness was in what to call my father. That word was, of course, too formal. Dad is what I had called Milton Walker, and Daddy seemed too juvenile. So on this visit, as on my first, I used no such term at all. Since then, I have tried out "Dad" a few times.

Toward the end of our afternoon there, we planted the gardenia and the chrysanthemum that we had brought them from Atlanta. Not in my father's garden out back, but on the side of the front yard, in a little space that was set aside for Mary's flowers, including several rose bushes.

And, of course, we walked in the garden, catching up on

what was doing well, what was suffering, how bad the pests were, the condition of the soil, the prospect for rain, heat.

We said our goodbyes and hit the road, a mess of gift collards in the car trunk, along with a few clumps of moss and several ferns from the back end of the garden.

After that first time, Lyn and I began regular trips back to Meridian. We have taken two of our five daughters (one of "hers," one of "mine"), both of whom were fascinated with the simple, rough antiquity of my father's garden.

Everyone's garden is magical. Each has the power to energize you when you think you have no energy left, to calm jangled nerves and to offset a bad-karma day. And each garden has unique properties, some of which are known only to the person who lives with it, some of which are apparent to everyone. When someone shares a garden with you, invites you in, it becomes more yours each time you go there. With each visit, it becomes more familiar, like a house you know or a person.

So it was with my father's garden.

By the time a couple of years had passed, my father's garden seemed much my own, made so by our visits and by the childhood memories they triggered. The topography, of course, was the same as I had known it decades earlier, as were most of the crops. I learned about his fertilizers, his well-worn but sturdy tools, and I got to know his Rube Goldberg irrigation system, a monument to plumbing ingenuity and to his esteem for water. At the back of the garden, some seventy-five feet from the house, he had perched a bathtub on cinderblocks, with a tube running from the drain all the way to the house. Rain filled the tub, and gravity pulled the water through the tube whenever he unplugged the drain.

A few feet from the tub, toward the vacant lot next door, is a drainage ditch which provides the most wonderful little black-spined ferns, along with several kinds of mosses. More-

Demonstrating homemade irrigation device.

When his garden was lush.

over, little toads play happily in this spot. Once, after collecting more ferns and mosses, I added a toad, fashioned a box with air holes to transport it back to Atlanta. As I loosed it when we arrived a little past midnight, Lyn said, "I bet he's heading right back to Meridian." I haven't seen him since, but I haven't given up on it yet.

Early in our visits we learned that if Lyn and I arrived later than we said we would, my father would be sitting on the front porch, wearing a logging company's gimme cap and a worried expression. "I thought y'all was coming at 2," he said one afternoon when we had dawdled along an Alabama back road, arriving close to 4 p.m. "I thought something had happened to y'all."

And, after a while, he came to expect the telephone calls that I began making soon after my first visit. One afternoon in early 1991, I telephoned after not having done so for maybe a month. Mary answered and told me my father had been very worried. "He was saying just the other day," she reported, "that just when he was getting to know his son, he stopped calling." Remembering my other two parents and how—after it was too late—I lamented not having kept in touch with them, I vowed to do better about calling my father. I did.

It was good to know that I had learned something in my half century of living. Fifty years. I marveled at reaching that mark in the spring of 1991. Where had the years gone? Wherever they went, they sure left a lot of changes with me.

Physically, I bounced back more slowly from a sprained ankle than I had twenty or even ten years earlier. I was still eating the way I always had—rich, fat, often fried—but unlike before, the food had begun to just lie there, turning into flab. The physical transformation, like going from summer to autumn, got my attention gently, but the emotional change was far more dramatic, like walking into an angry winter storm wearing shorts and a T-shirt.

One early, chilly emotional reality about reaching 50 was my wondering what a look from a woman meant. If she were younger than I, was she reminded of her father, her mentor, her lover? And if she were nearer my age, did she see in me maturity like hers and a respite from blue jeans and incomprehensible haircuts? Or was she just wondering why I didn't lose a few pounds and buy a toupee?

A young man never wonders why a woman is looking at him. His youthful arrogance tells him it's because she wants him as a lover. At fifty, wondering how a woman was responding to me, I was not trying to decide how and when we would bed down; I was trying to gauge where I fit—in society's eyes. Based on the response, I tried to determine how time had treated me, and how I had treated myself.

In short, how was I holding up? Did I look as if I felt old? Should my wife be proud to walk down the street with me? Of course, just one look from a stranger couldn't answer these questions, but it could give me a clue about what someone thought.

Women seem always to dread crossing over the fifth decade because they have been told the Big Lie: no matter how great you look at age fifty, you're still old. One woman friend believes women are made to feel older because, by fifty, most have stopped bearing children, "which is associated with usefulness. It's truly a different situation for men."

Perhaps, but at fifty, I, too, had no more children on my mind. Like most women my age, I had let go of that link to youth. And both men and women around fifty have had conversations like this:

Fiftyish: "You'll understand when you're my age."

Twentyish: "How old are you?"

"Fiftyish."

"Really? I didn't know you were that old."

That old. So much older and bigger than the skinny kid who joined the Army more than thirty years earlier and went off to grow up and see the world.

So, like many women, I approached fifty with trepidation, even though I knew that generally we men are perceived as mature at fifty, not old. Experienced, not worn out.

As April 15 rolled around, I heaved a sigh of relief. First of all, I had made it—not a small feat for a black man. My initial curiosity about how I appeared as a fifty-year-old gave way to some wonderful certainties about that time of life, which I view as a time of transition between youth and old age.

Life began feeling more precious than ever because I began feeling so profoundly that I had used up more of it than I had left. (There is irony in society's making Lyn feel older than it makes me feel, as statistics say she is likely to live longer than I will.)

Being fifty expanded my freedom to be friends with women by deflating the sexual tension that inevitably gets in the way of younger relationships. Yes, it is true that such tension will always exist, but, for me, being fifty meant I did not feel compelled to act on it in the way I might have at twenty.

That is one reason a pastime of watching my garden grow gardenias and azaleas and Japanese maples seems so much better than watching crowds grow at a nightclub. At twenty-five I was too unhappy and in too much of a hurry to garden. By fifty, fortunately, I had found Lyn and peace. Thus, the pace of growing and pruning pines suited me fine. A garden duplicates the stage for life's play. It changes through the seasons—sassy and colorful in April, beaten down and parched brown in August—and is akin to the flourishes and failures we experience over the years.

All in all, it felt great to be old enough to look back at good times I'd had around the world and, at the same time, young enough to look forward to new times in other exotic places— including a backyard garden.

Having learned that, in early 1992, I acknowledged to myself that I could no longer run the road in search of tragic news. As much as I liked my Los Angeles editor, Roger Smith, I had begun to dread hearing from him because too often that meant I'd have to rush to some place where misery was going on. So I told my people in Los Angeles I needed some thinking time, and we agreed on a two-month leave of absence. Stay or leave? I left. Less than a year before the *Los Angeles Times* offered an early retirement buyout for which I could have qualified. Timing is everything.

Lyn, of course, thought I had gone middle-age crazy, as she had just resigned from her job as spokeswoman for the mayor. She envisioned us sitting on the curb in front of our former home.

But everything happens the way it is supposed to. So during a visit to L.A. for a chat with editors, I had dinner with Steven Bochco, and he suggested that, since I was quitting a job without having another job, it looked as if I might have a little time to try my hand at writing a script for one of his television shows, "Civil Wars," about divorce court lawyers. Let him write what he knows, Steven must have been thinking.

Sure, I said, in the same way a politician runs for office, not really believing he'll win—then, when he does, he wakes up, slaps his head and says, "Oh, God, what do I do now?"

That was my reaction when Steven telephoned me in Atlanta weeks later and asked if I were ready to come to Los Angeles for a script meeting. Sensing my doubt, he said, reassuringly, "Don't worry about it. The worst you can do is screw it up." Hmmmmm. The script made air, and as usual with Steven's productions, by the time it did, it was something to be proud of.

By the summer of 1992, I had figured out that journalism still wasn't through with me, but it couldn't work unless I worked off the road. So I applied for an editor's job at the *Atlanta Journal-Constitution*, as the combined papers had been named, and returned to the building at 72 Marietta Street in July.

"Hey, Lee," said a guard, whom I had not seen in a dozen years—as if we had just spoken the day before. That was good.

Good, too, from the start were my gardening conversations with colleagues, old and new. Always ready to chat and share experiences was longtime columnist Celestine Sibley, whose gentle, vibrant writings and passionate gardening always inspired. And her surprise plant offerings, including the cream and green ivy from her home grounds (I call it "Celestine") have been pleasurable additions to our space.

But editing and I were not good together; I missed writing. Now that I was living an increasingly softer life, away from the madding bars, juke joints and wild streets, features appealed to me, as opposed to news. Switching from editing to writing in early 1993, I immediately began producing pieces about gardening. And by midyear, I was offered the opportunity to write a gardening column. Thus was I thrown into the briar patch.

Finally, my professional and personal lives were integrated. I was writing about what I lived.

Gardening, of course, was what had insured a relationship between my father and me. And as I was going through my changes from news man to gardening man (or "the gardening guy," as one teenage student called me during my chat with a class), I developed a greater and greater appreciation for the pastime-passion and for my father's long, deep connection to it.

During our visits to Meridian, I hungrily ate up information about this simple man who thought simple but powerful thoughts, expressing them with moral but unsanctimonious certainty. His memory was fading, so there was much I would never know about him, his family, his life. But much was left, too.

I learned that my father had a daughter (not with my mother), Christine, who is twelve years older than I am and lives in Alabama. She and I have had good talks and plan to meet. I learned too that my father is seriously religious. A Baptist churchgoer, he sits on the porch and talks about Biblical characters as if they lived next door. He and Mary get into heated arguments about the proper interpretation of the Word and how it should be applied to life in these times. References to the Lord and to the inevitability of His will permeate their conversations.

One day the four of us were sitting on the porch talking about one of California's earthquakes. "I hate to see those people get killed," Mary said, "but there's nothing you can do about it. The Lord's in charge."

"You can stay at home," retorted my father, his sense of humor and connection to home bursting through his religion. "Everytime you go out there, you take a chance on something happening to you."

Humor runs through him. Like many folks who never have held a driver's license, my father is a consummate back-seat driver. After directing me the wrong way on a one-way street during bill-paying runs to the gas and water companies, he quipped, "If they arrest me, I'll just say we was only going one way."

During one of our visits, he told a wonderful childhood story about why his name is spelled Mae, and mine is May.

Seems when he was a young man, a cousin convinced him that May is a month, while Mae is a name. So my father changed his spelling but later gave me the one used by the rest of his family.

Since our first meeting, we have dug deeper and deeper, mining years-buried information like that so often lost in families, especially those divided by divorce and distance.

Surprising to me, he had kept up loosely with my journalism career, mentioning stories I had covered, foreign lands I had visited, television shots of me scribbling notes near some newsmaker.

I've heard stories that portray our ancestors as proud and loving, including those about my father's mother, Cora, who first inspired him to garden. He recalled memories of his childhood home in our ancestral western Alabama, a home in which howling winds knifed through spaces between the logs. But his mother made him a quilt, he recalled, adding, simply, "She loved me."

My father's recollections never seem bitter, even when he told the story of the white man who tried to make his grandmother cross a stream, flogging her and causing permanent disabilities after she refused.

Even as he recalled the era of separate water fountains, backs of buses and separately unequal schools, he never seemed dispirited by the memories—quite a feat for a black man his age who has lived his entire life in Alabama and Mississippi. In fact, his proud, calm demeanor and firm eyes speak self-confidence that defies all racist efforts to make him feel less than a man.

And for him, part of being a man, a huge part, always has been paying your way, earning what you get, getting what you deserve, neither seeking nor accepting handouts. He said, "You go down to some of these places to buy something or pay a water bill or a light bill and you're short a couple of pennies. They might let you by, but they're gonna remember it. They're not gonna say that's all right; you're gonna have to pay whenever you go back down there again. They ain't never told me, 'You don't have to pay,' and I never did ask 'em to. When I go down there, I know how they is, and when they give me my change, I want all of mine. I got just as much right to want all of mine as they is to want all of theirs."

Uneducated in the formal sense, my father learned that all honest work has value, taking great pride in his career as a plumber.

That profession occupied most of his adult life, until he reached retirement age. Years later, he still spoke passionately of his hard work and hard-won skill in his craft. Like a surgeon recalling a particularly interesting challenge in the operating room, he told me of some cold winter back in the 1960s, when pipes were breaking off and how he devised a way to replace them before the thawed water could gush through folks' floors.

He gardened always. Recalling long days of lugging tools and connecting pipes, he said, "No matter how tired I was when I came home, I'd go out there and dig and plant. I never did let nothing keep me out of that garden."

Land was prized right up there with water, both inextricably bound to the welfare of people. Thus, it was not surprising that my father found my ornamental gardening somewhat puzzling.

As we walked among his lush butter beans and peas and okra one day in 1992, our talk turned to my space in southwest Atlanta.

"What are you growing in your garden?" he said, stooping to pull an offending weed.

"Rhododendron, Japanese black pines, azaleas, Japanese maples, bamboo, ferns and a lot of other plants," I said.

"Uh huh," said my father, "but what do you grow for food?"

"Well, there's rosemary, sage, thyme, cilantro and a few other herbs."

Chuckling, he just shook his head and reached for a hoe, so he could do some weeding around the corn, something worth fooling with.

It was a nice moment, one of many we've had since June of 1989. That moment was a way of defining the differences in our generations and economic lots in life. My father, like many people his age, always saw gardening as a necessity, a way of raising food that he couldn't afford to buy, while many people my age began gardening not just for food, sometimes growing no food at all, but growing plants for the sheer pleasure they bring.

The moment also was a metaphor for our relationship; we were growing different crops, but they, and we, were undeniably kin.

* * *

Just as gardening gave my father and me the tools to build a relationship, it formed the foundation for relationships with countless other people as well. I've found no better bridge to people than gardening. Neither my father nor my Dad nor Mother ever said that. But I know they knew it.

I have learned something else that my parents always knew but never said: It's just about impossible to find a gardener who is a bad person, even an ornamental gardener. And I have come to know that a garden is many things beyond a place to grow food or flowers. Sanctuary, exercise room, meditation place. It is all those things and more.

And everyone sees in a garden, as in life, what she wants to see.

During a tour of our garden, a young woman said to Lyn, "I know now what kind of man I want. I want a man who is a gardener. Any man patient enough to make all these plants grow and thrive is patient enough to sustain a relationship."

As a gardening man, I loved the sentiment, even though I know the facts of gardening can try any man's soul.

In any case, a garden is a font of information, inspiration and wisdom. This realization, unspoken for most of my life, has guided me through hard times and bad times, and into some incredibly good times.

Increasingly, gardening has been a connection to people—some of them people I'd long known but not as friends until we discovered this common interest. When I lived in Atlanta the first time, gardening rarely was a basis for friendship. But gardening has been an absolute friendly glue time after time during my second go-round in Atlanta, making it clear that, not only had the city changed, so had I.

I have met strangers, too, through gardening. Sometimes in strange ways.

At a nursery one delicious late-spring day, a woman and I

struck up a conversation about Indian hawthorn while waiting in the checkout line, admiring its lovely pink blossoms and its shiny new leaves, copper-colored.

Somehow we got from there to oakleaf hydrangea, comparing stories about ours and rhapsodizing about how we love the leaves' autumn colors of wine and gold as much as we love the great bunches of white blooms in spring. As we were leaving, she suggested that I follow her home to see her hydrangeas and other plants.

Sure, I said. Minutes later, we both pulled up in the driveway and immediately set out examining the shrubs. She really did have some big ones. Tall, too. They were lovely.

Pretty soon, the woman's husband appeared at the front door. We introduced ourselves, and he disappeared, leaving his wife and me to admire alone. At that moment, our differing races were shunted aside, something all too rare. A black man and a white woman we were, yes. But more important, we were two people in love with nature and joined by it.

My ties to gardening go way back, way deep and have included many people. But my closest connection to this passionate pastime is Lyn.

And while that has been so ever since we met, the truth of it was never so evident as it became after my father and I reunited and I saw the power of gardening as a building block for relationships of all kinds. That power has not been lost on Lyn and me. We talk about it and through it more deeply appreciate our own togetherness.

Lyn and I are so connected through gardening that, when I do not garden regularly, she suffers. In the summer of 1994, there was record rainfall in Georgia. I barely touched the earth during the month of July, prompting Lyn to ask if I had fallen out of love with gardening. No, I explained. The rain did my watering for me, and the mosquitoes kept me from enjoying the lush results. Only when I was back out there with a hose pipe and an appreciative eye was she truly convinced, though.

Just as Mother and Dad had given me a loving childhood that allowed me to meet my father on peaceful, happy terms, Lyn helped me intensify my love of life—and gardening—in adulthood. Often in our early years, she and I wondered how we would have been together had we met, say, twenty years before we did. Each time we wonder, we conclude that our relationship might not have lasted, just as my other two marriages did not. We were both different then. Things bloom when they're supposed to.

Maybe that is how it is with my father. Who knows how we might have got on had we met, re-met, twenty years earlier? We would not have been the same two people. For one thing, there was no Lyn in my life then. For another, I was not nearly the gardener I had become by the time we did get together again.

And so Lyn and I appreciate our present, not lamenting our past.

On some days, the chief event for us is a "tour," my showing her around the garden after I have spent hours putting in new plants or moving old ones around. Cradling a Bombay and tonic during hot times or a Jack Daniel's in the chill, we stroll and commune, noting the changes, marveling at new growth and shouting, "Sighting! Sighting!" whenever one of us first spies a new bloom. Sometimes we turn on that old record album, Miles's *Sketches of Spain*, that I bought as a child soldier, and hear the hauntingly lyrical "Concierto de Aranjuez" floating out through the windows. Or Grieg's evocative, woodsy "Peer Gynt" or B.B., Ella, Aretha, Billie, or Patsy telling us how she falls to pieces. Much of our music is part of our separate pasts. Now in a combined collection, it is an important part of our life together.

The garden creates its own sounds, too. In fact, there is a garden within the garden. It is the sound garden.

When it is warm enough in spring and cool enough in

A garden requires much work, but sometimes it just needs enjoying.

autumn to open windows and doors, we can hear the wind rustle the bamboo leaves. The sound is dry and slightly crackly during soft breezes, resembling thin whistles when the wind picks up.

The grasses behave much like the bamboo. The higher the wind, the more likely it is that they can be heard. Two green clumps in the back sing greetings to us during garden strolls. Another clump, red and green, in a window box outside the front parlor begs to have the window opened. When it is, the dancing leaves of grass entertain and intrigue.

Just as a bonsai—a miniaturized tree, a rock, some moss in a tray—represents a much larger scene in nature, this grass whispering in the wind takes me to a peaceful, comforting vista I love: waving, whispering sea grasses in places like the islands off Georgia and Cape Ann, Massachusetts. These huge expanses of grasses rise and fall with the tide. My clump in a window box asserts itself with the rise and fall of my window.

Far less elegantly, the oak next door, believed to predate the Civil War, tosses acorns down onto our roof and porches with power, petulance and incredible frequency, like a million squirrels bent on mischief (I know the rodents take aim at people, throwing whatever they happen to be eating; one tossed a glob of potato salad at Lyn and me soon after we moved in). The rat-a-tat-tat acorn sounds, too, belong; they are part of fall's garden.

At the other end of the spectrum are the falling leaves. In moments of true calm and quiet concentration, I can hear them as they touch down, piling onto others or scraping a bench or rock.

Here, too, there is a range of intensity, from the barely audible tulip tree and dogwood leaves to the relatively raucous ones from the saucer magnolia.

In the spring of 1994, when we had to pare down the household of Lyn's mother and move her to an elder care home, we discovered a brass disk, about a foot and a half wide, with mysterious markings. We do not know which country among many she traveled provided this memento. Nor do we know what memories it recalls. And as Alzheimer's has her, she cannot tell us.

Whatever its origin, the plate now gives wonderful form and function in the sound garden. I hung the disk on a hook against a brick wall out back. Whenever it catches a breeze, it gongs. Sometimes softly, once or twice, like the low whistle of a train that beckons in the night, calling me to get on board, as Edna St. Vincent Millay wrote, "No matter where it's going."

At other times, in high winds, the plate gongs and bongs harder, longer, more persistently, like a warning. Maybe it simply says, Listen. Hear.

We do. Each morning, we try to spend at least a few minutes appreciating nature's presentations before we dash off to work. Some mornings that means no more than sniffing the rose that rests on the arbor near the back gate, or touching the moss that grows around a bonsai or listening to the cheery greetings of birds attracted to the garden, or just catching a glimpse of the goldfish in our tiny pond. On others it means a long look at both the front and back, with a few minutes to

A little time each day to see, hear, smell and feel the garden.

listen to the tsukubai water streaming through bamboo onto stone.

In the evenings, when we are less pressed, we often sit on the back deck and take meals or lounge on the front porch and just be. On some of those evenings, inside brick walls, sheltered by thick shrubs and trees, enveloped by fragrance from native azalea or banana shrub or ginger lily or sweet olive, we lie down, crushing the spearmint and the lavender, releasing their scents, too, doing much more than just being.

I think I would never have become an outdoor grilling man if I hadn't figured out that I could slap a few chops on the hibachi and gaze out onto the back garden. My starting to like the process of putting fire to meat has improved my status as a mate immeasurably.

While Lyn does not dig the holes or plant plants (she calls the entire process exotic, mysterious and beyond her ken), she certainly does her part to help build the garden; she is a great appreciator, and often a muse and a critic, always a supporter.

In the spring of 1992, I needed to replace our Korean boxwoods with the old-fashioned English ones. Had to have that fragrance, the one that reminds some of cat pee but is nectar to my nose. So I looked all over the Atlanta area to no avail. Bad timing; sometimes it seems nobody is selling what you want when you want it. Lyn suggested that I try one of the plantations in southern Virginia, as they make livings on historical homes landscaped with man-high boxwoods. Surely they'd have a few for sale, she said, having remembered seeing them years earlier when she visited the state to shoot a story for her television travel series.

I shopped by telephone, and happily, I found a place in Charles City, between Richmond and Norfolk, a plantation, that did, indeed, sell English boxwoods, propagated on the plantation.

As it happens, we were scheduled to attend a niece's wedding in New Jersey a week or so after I made my telephonic discovery. What added incentive I had for enjoying pomp and matrimony! I do recall waiting until vows had been said and champagne drunk before revving up our Honda and hitting I-95 South.

In Charles City, the day was cool and misty, perfect for plant-buying. After selecting twenty boxwoods, fifteen small ones and five medium-sized ones, we stuffed them into the little car, leaving barely enough room for ourselves. Lyn, who is far more likely to tear up with joy over a wedding than over a boxwood, was moved by my obvious happiness. "My enduring picture of you is you sitting in that little car, surrounded by twenty boxwoods," she said later.

Lyn also was there during my first hunt for garden rocks. Needing a few boulders, I looked in the yellow pages and found a place that sold them. Five hundred-, six hundred-, fifteen hundred-pound stones piled up for display and perusal like giant-sized produce in a supermarket.

After much clambering and examining, I picked out three, ranging from about one hundred pounds up to about eight hundred, had them loaded onto a flatbed truck and hauled to our home in Atlanta, about sixty miles away. (The price of the rocks was reasonable, if you have to buy rocks at all—about ten cents a pound. The more serious money came in transportation cost, more than a hundred dollars for that first haul.) Lyn

Baby boxwoods delight planter Lee.

watched this business in supportive but stunned silence, amazed that she was married to a man on a rock-buying mission.

The flatbed, with rocks and a forklift to unload them, roared up to our house, attracting a few curious stares in the neighborhood, and inspiring one neighbor to quip: "Betcha nobody's gonna steal any of these."

Most of our gardening drives have been serendipitous, jaunts down back roads where I spy a half-hidden nursery stocking unusual plants at unusually reasonable prices. During one such trip, we happened upon a man near Cartersville, Georgia, who specialized in (was addicted to) day lilies, a passion he indulged freely in the wake of his retirement from the federal government.

Poking around his rambling property, on which he also grew shrubs and trees for sale, I wondered if he had the same problems as I did with squirrels digging up every other newly planted seedling. So I asked, "What do you do about squirrels? How do you deal with the little varmints trying to undo everything that you do?"

In a drawl dripping with humor, the old man gave me perhaps the best answer I've ever gotten to this crucial question:

"Pet 'em."

Yes, I've tried a million anti-squirrel remedies, including sprinkling red pepper in their paths, Tabasco on plant leaves and spreading used cat litter around plants (I'd heard that somebody in California used mountain-lion urine to scare the rodents away, so I was trying the closest thing I had to that). But in the end, the little devils just keep coming back. Thus, I have learned that, with squirrels as with so many other problems in life, sometimes there is nothing to do but adapt.

Gardening experiences—mine and others'—have given me great hope for the changes that digging in the dirt can uncover.

"I was seven or eight years old when I started working in the field," my father told me one summer day in 1994 as we sat on his porch, sipping soft drinks, or "soda water," as he calls it. Working in the field at his backwoods birthplace in Choctaw County, Alabama. "I wasn't big enough to hoe a row at first," he said. "But my mama gave me a little short-handled hoe and put me in there with the stumps and bushes. Mama knew I couldn't hurt that stump. She put me where I couldn't hurt nothin'. Only thing I could do was good.

"Old people were that way; they could always find somethin' you could do. You weren't gon' just sit down there and look at them. You were gon' do somethin'."

What he did was whatever he could—at first, mostly weeding—to help grow the family food, including peas, greens, butter beans, corn, okra and sorghum cane. They'd grind the cane and make syrup from it.

He loves the memory of self-sufficiency, something that carried into other parts of his life. "We learned how to eat what we could get," he said. "They couldn't starve me 'cause I could eat anything anybody else could eat. If we didn't have nothing but peas and bread, I'd eat that."

Like so many people in his generation, my father depended on the soil for his independence. He and his family grew most of what they ate. That is changing—more in the South than in other parts of the country.

Sadly, I read about how Southerners these days are less likely than their ancestors to grow food or flowers. And that Northerners are more likely than Southerners to have both vegetable and flower gardens.

This is the other side of progress. People like my father and his parents did not have the money to buy food or flowers in stores and markets, so they had to grow them. Now all this stuff is lined up at the market.

While this makes life easier in some ways, it is at the same time such a sad loss. A loss of independence, of connections to nature, a loss of unfooled-with food. Losing the will or desire to garden is, perhaps, an indication of how far we are willing to go to shuck off our agrarian image. In the process, however, we discard some of life's wonderful simplicity.

That's my view, but as a group black people are less likely than white people to grow food or flowers. For many, getting away from gardening is much like getting away from the blues. Friends tell me that both bring back too many images of the days when black people were slaves, then underpaid and underprotected field hands who dug, planted, weeded and harvested because they had to. I understand those images, but for me they are overshadowed by the beauty and joy and good times I get from digging in my ground when I feel like it.

My father's story of hanging out in the fields as a young boy is instructive in many ways.

Not only did he establish a connection with nature at a very young age, but he also became connected to people in a pro-found way. Getting to know him and many other gardeners, I have come to believe that the act of growing something—working dirt, sowing seeds, pruning, weeding, harvesting—somehow helps people appreciate other people. Maybe it's the naturalness of gardening, its statement that says plants and people share and grow on this earth. For sure, gardening as a shared experience gives gardeners much to talk about, ways to relate.

What a gift gardening can be for children. What better way to teach them the lessons of success and failure in life, respect for nature, self-sufficiency, gentleness, the value and beauty of a space free of discarded candy bags, soda cans and hamburger wrappers. Once a child (or an adult) tends a garden, trashing the ground becomes difficult.

I have seen the power of the idea of gardening reflected in children's eyes, and I love it; it shines in such delightful contrast to the dead eyes that stare hollowly from so many young heads.

On Halloween night, Lyn and I often sit in the porch swing and gleefully greet the trick-or-treaters. I've been pleased and amazed at the attention and compliments so many of them pay to the garden. And, more amazing, at how many call it a garden. At seven and eight years old, an age when it was still a yard to me. These children are ripe for gardening.

As a guest in 1994 at Hubert Elementary School in southeast Atlanta, I talked about my career as a newspaper writer, my educational background, family—the usual motivational material. The young group was politely attentive. But when I turned to specifics I had written about in gardening columns, including certain trees, herbs, shrubs and vegetables, they absolutely lit up.

At one point I mentioned that American Indians once used twigs from the dogwood tree as toothbrushes. Immediately one young man flipped through his dictionary to the tree name and dashed up to point out the definition and illustration to me. We went on to azaleas, to roses and tomatoes and honeysuckles and others, learning each time to spell the plant name and to talk about its taste and beauty and how useful it has been to people.

As so often happens, many of the youngsters cited a grandmother or grandfather who "grows things." They seemed proud.

I loved the connectedness I heard, and I felt the students

did, too. It was a connection not just to the plants (some of which they were growing in a school garden), but to people, present and past. If they become gardeners, they will dig in the dirt in much the same way their ancestors did, grow okra and camellias in much the same way and, I hope, be strong in the same way so many early Americans had to be.

Closer to home, too, I have tried to make that point. Among our blended group of five daughters, Leslie is the only one who has lived in the same city with us. Fortunately for her, she loves gardening. Otherwise, she would be terribly bored at being given cuttings of corkscrew willow to take home.

Far from bored, Leslie had become a terrific gardener-in-training by the time she reached her thirtieth year. And, on occasion, the keeper of the family's historical plant stock.

An example: the Jerusalem cherry that I grew as a young man at my parents' home in East St. Louis remained there long after I moved away. During one of my visits from Washington in the mid-1980s, I noticed the plant and harvested several pieces of its orange-colored fruit, from which I grew the little shrub again.

Soon after Lyn and I moved to Atlanta, white flies brutalized the plant, which was growing indoors. Instead of fighting the flies, I decided to pitch the plant. But first, I gave Leslie some of its fruit, which she planted, creating her own shrub and keeping the chain alive. We named it for my mother: Riller.

Trying to mold gardeners at an ever younger age, I influence our grandchildren every chance I get, ever since I became a brand-new grandfather in Washington, where daughter Cami and her husband, John, visited us in the mid-'80s with baby Lauren Michael. Before she was walking, we had her over at the U.S. Botanic Garden, admiring the plant scenery, exotic and ordinary. Already attuned to the specialness of a plant, she reached out her little hand, ever so gently, and touched the tip of a leaf, barely. Then she looked at me and smiled. Talk about happy-making. That was. And when her sister Kate came

Grandlee with Lauren Michael at the Botanic Garden.

along, that doubled the pass-on possibilities for Grandlee.

Some day, a long time away, I trust one of them will say to a daughter or son, "I was seven or eight years old when I started working in the garden . . ."

When I first visited my father in 1989 and told other family members about it, Leslie said, "That shows you should never let people go." She is right. If you care about someone, it is never too late to make contact.

I keep hoping that someday my two younger daughters will come around. By the 1990s, we were exchanging letters and telephone calls from time to time, and I have met them at neutral places like clothing stores to buy for them once in a while (a modified version of the McDonald's Daddy). And one of them actually came to my home during a visit to the city. It was a tentative visit, one I had urged for years.

My daughter seemed calm, but she was not curious about my new life—and certainly not about my garden (gardening genes are not necessarily inherited). I was happy to see her at my home but sad to know she might never feel it was hers, too. Maybe my father had similar feelings at first. Someday, maybe, when they are older, I will know my daughters as I have gotten to know my father, and they will know me.

Once established, a long-lost relationship is, in at least one way, like all others: it has to be nurtured, worked at. And, sometimes still there are disappointments.

I had hoped, at some point, my father would visit our home in Atlanta. I wanted him to see my garden, my home. We had talked about that for a couple of years, and in the summer of 1993 I mailed him a round-trip bus ticket. A few days before he was to travel, he decided he did not feel well enough, expressing fear that he would fall deathly ill on the bus. I suggested driving over and bringing him back, but a car was not much better than a bus, he felt, and he wasn't about to fly.

Having known a lot of older people who don't want to leave home, I would have understood, even if he had not been ill. At thirty-two years his junior, I often find it difficult to leave home.

But it was clear that he was going down.

Just after his eighty-fourth birthday, which was May 16, 1993, Lyn and I drove to Meridian to see him and Mary. For the first time, we saw a mostly barren space where the garden normally flourished that time of year. A few garlic plants and an old grapevine were just about the only signs of garden life. In telephone conversations he had mentioned not feeling well and being under a doctor's care for high blood pressure. To be sure, the man we saw then was frail and unsteady compared with the one I remember wielding the hoe and the BB gun with equal zest and sureness.

A realist to the bone, my father was quick to acknowledge the change.

"Ain't no good to say I'm good as I used to be," he said. "Any man my age thinks that, it's 'cause he ain't never done nothin'."

Frailty may have kept him from gardening, but not from talking about it.

He said the hobby comes naturally because, "Momma always had a garden." Over the years, he learned that gardening "exercises every muscle a man got in his body."

I smiled as I listened, thinking I could just as easily have been the speaker.

Seeing a father going down slow is always tough. Watching Dad disappear into death in 1977 wrenched my soul. I had known him longer and better than I have known my birth father and thus had more experiences to lose when he died.

But seeing my birth father confront physical decline so soon after we had begun building a relationship brought its own special pain. So many questions remained unanswered. And so many years—a time when he was young, healthy and strong—passed before we tried to know each other. Neither of us spoke of that, however. And never will.

So on that visit and since, we talked about gardening. But that touches on other feelings and fears.

As we kicked through the dusty grayness of my father's virtually empty, sun-baked garden, he answered my question about whether he might plant again: "When a man gets my age, he can't plan on nothing for the future. All I can do is hope."

Just before Lyn and I left, he put together a starter package for me: okra and watermelon seeds, a handful of corn kernels, some peanuts. All in a little white cardboard can, with a red plastic top.

"You can get a good crop out of these," he said, forgetting or ignoring my bent toward ornamental gardening.

I brought the seeds home and stored them in the wild shed that is filled with gardening tools and disorder, knowing that one day I might grow food as my father had—and hoping that some day soon he would again.

In the spring of 1994, I took the can out of the shed and checked its contents. Looking good. This would be the year. For the first time in well over a decade, I would grow food again, using some of the Ples Mae seeds.

When the ground warmed enough, around Easter, I sowed. I knew I would not be growing watermelon or corn or peanuts in my small space. But the Ples okra went on the high side of the back garden, so sunny I call it Sahara, between the barberry and the loquat. More okra went in a pot on the back deck. Inspired, I bought other food plants. A few collard plants went in near a stand of nandina. Cayenne peppers moved into the quince neighborhood. Eggplant seedlings found a home near the spirea. Tomatoes I grew in pots, and one in the ground wound its way onto a tree-form wisteria.

On the telephone I told my father about my foray into food-growing. He did not seem surprised. I did not bother to tell him that part of the way I convinced myself to grow food again was to contemplate the beauty of some vegetable plants.

The eggplant, for example, grows a wonderful rich purple, and pepper, in addition to satisfying my addiction to spices, give a space great reds, yellows and greens. The foliage on both is attractive, as are okra's blossoms.

Perhaps I need not have told my father any of this. All along, I had assumed he was growing food just for his stomach. Maybe it was for his eyes, too. I know it was for his soul.

In any case, when we talked, it was mostly about the advantages of growing our own: big flavor and little pesticide. "When you go to the market and pick up something, you don't know what you're getting," he said. "Even the store people don't know what's in it."

I wasn't sure if he'd ever eaten a store-bought tomato, and I made a vow not to, either.

My father was supportive, and characteristically, he lauded the hard work and reward connected to planting. "Nothin's gonna come and get in your lap," he said. "You got to work for it." And he shared some wisdom that I kept in mind as I rejoined the ranks of vegetable people: "It's a risky run any way you go. Always be prepared to go back over it again if you mess up; if you fail, just plant again."

As for my father's garden, it lay mostly fallow again in 1994. Only the garlic plants peeped out of the gray ground. He said he ate the garlic for health reasons. And, way in the back, the grapevine grew, forlorn. The wonderful bathtub irrigation system was dismantled; he said he gave it to a friend for scrap.

Still it was a garden. Tilled by "a fella I know" and divided into neat rows. And as in each spring since we re-met in 1989, we walked in the space, and talked. Truly, when wound up, he always turns into a walking, talking compendium of advice on life and gardening.

Noting how much rain there had been, he warned, "It's better to work in the ground when it's a little too dry than when it's too wet. A person's gotta know when to stay outta a garden as well as when to go in one."

He stopped to pull weeds, rearing back and straining mightily, making me nervous, as he grabbed one, then a second, then a third, grunting and flinging them to the ground. "You have to let 'em know they ain't welcome," he said firmly. And he talked on: "Everybody's full of mistakes, and ain't no need for nobody to think they ain't, neither. A person who thinks he don't make no mistakes—you'll never learn that person nothin'. A man who ain't never done nothing wrong ain't never done nothin'."

My father has come up with so many of these gardening-life messages that, over the years, I have listed some:

— Gardening is a risk to run. Some years you win. Some years you gonna lose.

— A garden and a home are for people who got patience.

— You learn more from your own mistakes and successes than you can learn from gardening magazines.

— Be skeptical.

— Some people try to lead when they oughta be following somebody else.

— If the blind lead the blind, they all gonna fall in the ditch.

— A man who tills the soil is gonna eat the bread.

— Sometime you have to crawl in place of walking.

— It's always a blessing to get to the place you started out for.

— A man lives and learns. At least he suppose to.

— I learned not to want the stuff I can't have.

— Ain't no man spose to just sit up and let other people work for him.

— I don't care how many millions of dollars you got, some way or another, every once in a while, you gonna sweat.

— The Bible says trouble come like the leaves on trees. If yours ain't come like that yet, you oughta feel like you doing a hundred.

— Man needn't think he's gonna live in a flower bed.

— Don't plant on no sign or no seasons. Plant in the ground.

— Some people don't want to get old, and they don't want to die. You got to do one or the other.

I have heard these bits of advice over and over since 1989, gathering them as we walked. During our early visits, we admired the sturdy vegetables, then later, we kicked along the empty rows. Out of the dust and the mud of our many walks, under broiling sun and cloudy skies, a garden and a man's body both declined. But a kinship grew. It is a most bountiful harvest.

My father is not given to sentimental expressions, although Lyn and I believe we saw a tear in his eye as we pulled away from the house one day. But in one of our telephone conversations in mid-1994, after we had discussed the rain and the sun and our hopes for gardening the next spring, he said, "A man is blessed when he got a child who cares something about him. Some children these days don't care nothing about their parents."

"I know," I said. "I love you, Dad."

"I love you too. Goodbye, son."

Deep South Books

The University of Alabama Press